Contents

List of tables

List of figures

Airports
and Planning

KENNETH R. SEALY

Theory and Practice in Geography

OXFORD UNIVERSITY PRESS

Oxford University Press, Ely House, London W.1

OXFORD LONDON GLASGOW NEW YORK
TORONTO MELBOURNE WELLINGTON CAPE TOWN
IBADAN NAIROBI DAR ES SALAAM LUSAKA ADDIS ABABA
KUALA LUMPUR SINGAPORE JAKARTA HONG KONG TOKYO
DELHI BOMBAY CALCUTTA MADRAS KARACHI

ISBN 0 19 874041 7

© Oxford University Press 1976

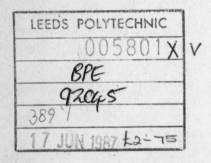
Printed in Great Britain
by J. W. Arrowsmith Ltd., Bristol

1 Introduction

We live in a tumultuous age in which the discoveries of science, applied through technology, have produced a social and economic revolution that we have only begun to understand. Actions by individuals, or by public bodies, may now profoundly affect the lives and environment of the rest of the community. Aviation is a good example of rapid technological change, and the airports that serve it are key elements in its development. The barnstormers of the 1920s were ephemeral, the airports of the 1930s affected the local area, Heathrow was conceived as a London airport, but the projected Third London Airport—despite its name—is a project of national and international importance. It is significant too that, although work on the Maplin site is suspended, no ultimate decision regarding its future has been taken after a decade of intensive thought and work.

Aviation is a spatial activity concerned with supplying a transport service: a derived demand arising from the need to match the production of goods and services with their points of consumption. Sometimes the canvas seems very broad, and we may contemplate whether any spatial optimum is possible within existing national boundaries, or whether planning should embrace larger units such as the European Economic Community. Aviation is, then, a matter of interest to the geographer.

Modern development is more and more concerned with alternative solutions to planning problems, and this implies a more refined look at the consequences of particular policies. Without standards of reference, decisions tend to be local, and their consequences ill-defined. The present airport system in this country is a good example of a spatial distribution resulting from an amalgam of small decisions made over time. Then again, airports are expensive to build and maintain, so that the effects of past decisions are long-lived; indeed many people feel that we are stuck with the present system for a considerable time to come, and that the best that we can do is to modify it for present and future use.

Not all aspects of the subject are of equal interest, but care must be taken before dismissing any of them. Airport ownership may, for example, seem a marginal element with respect to distribution but, as we shall try to show, airport provision may vary according to whether a national plan, or a *laissez-faire* approach, is adopted.

Here is a challenging field—the more so as an increasing mass of information becomes available and concepts and techniques to use it proliferate. In particular, we are planning in an era when what happens tomorrow need not resemble today. Yet we often have only today upon which to build our models, and so have to make assumptions that are vulnerable. The analysis of travel demand undertaken for the Commission on the Third London Airport has already been overtaken by the fuel crisis, by inflation, and by changes in the pattern of traffic at airports like Gatwick— to name only some of the changes since 1970. Care is needed in the use of models to ensure that their limitations are clearly stated. Strong words have been written about theoretical approaches to airline regulation, or rather de-regulation. Certainly we are faced with a rapidly developing technology. What, we may well ponder, will be the spatial repercussions when aircraft take off from holes in the ground in city centres, carry 500 people, and cruise at Mach 3.0 for 16 000 km? Amongst other things, such a possibility would mean roughly six times the annual working capacity of a current Boeing 747, which itself represents a three-fold increase over the *Queen Mary* of the ocean liner era.

This book cannot wholly comprehend so wide a subject, and a catholic choice has had to be made with the aim of demonstrating some of the more vital elements. For this reason readers should make use of the reference material, much of which, as it happens, is not geographical in origin. This may perhaps suggest laxity on the part of geographers, but more practically it indicates the inter-disciplinary nature of studies in air transport. The technical development of the aircraft is a high priority, and here Stratford's book (1973) on air transport economics brings out the influence of technical matters very clearly. Many of the papers in the *Aeronautical Journal* of the Royal Aeronautical Society are also very useful sources. The reader might well begin by reading Sir Morien Morgan's fascinating account of the early development of the supersonic airliner which led to the evolution of Concorde (Morgan 1972). As we shall see in the final chapter, many of the studies of the social and economic consequences of that aircraft are filled with doubt.

In detail, Chapter 2 looks at the airport as a unit, and tries to identify and discuss some of the problems of siting and development, including the wider environmental aspects. Chapter 3 takes a strategic viewpoint and considers the case for national planning, as well as the alternative competitive pricing model. Chapter 4 deals with British airport planning, while the final chapter takes a very tentative look at the future, both in the short term, and over a longer span of time.

References

Morgan, Sir Morien (1972) 'A new shape in the sky', *Aeron. Jnl.*, 76, 1.
Stratford, A. H. (1973) *Air Transport Economics in the supersonic era*, 2nd edn., London.
Stratford and Associates (1974), *Northern Region Airport Study*, Maidenhead.

2 Airport planning

Introduction

An airport's main function is to facilitate the movement of passengers and goods by air, but in order to do this it must not only provide adequate terminal facilities to expedite the trans-shipment of traffic from surface to air transport, but must also provide for the safe operation of the aircraft and surface vehicles involved. To carry out these functions, the airport site must satisfy some very stringent demands—not the least of which will concern the actual acreage of land required. Fixed-wing aircraft are great space users: a Boeing 747 not only needs a 3000 m. runway space, but because of the aircraft's cruciform shape, it occupies 4200 sq. m. of standing space, not allowing for any space needed for movement. Finally, an airport affects the surrounding area, so that account must also be taken of environmental effects.

The major factors determining the siting of airports may be summarized:
1. Availability of land
2. Terrain and meteorological conditions
     (i) Nature of sites; economy of construction
     (ii) Local meteorological conditions
3. Relationship to air transport requirements
     (i) Pattern of routes and traffic   (iii) Air Traffic Control
     (ii) Presence of other airports   (iv) Passenger/cargo catchments
4. Access to surface transport
     (i) Characteristics of local/national systems as they affect the site
5. Obstructions
     (i) Buildings, power lines   (ii) Noise abatement
6. Utilities—Water, drainage, oil
7. Environmental factors
     (i) Economic effects on incomes, employment
     (ii) Social effects of noise; obstruction and the quality of the
          environment.

Such a list provides an envelope from which more systematic relationships may be drawn up.

First we may take an over-all view of the airport problem by considering the airport as a system in contact with a surrounding universe. Such a picture is attempted in Fig. 1 which brings in not only the elements already noted, but also includes wider issues of ownership and control. Within this frame a number of interrelated sub-systems may be discerned, for example the movement of passengers and freight from their ultimate origins in the surrounding region, through the terminal, to the aircraft and the outgoing airline system. This chain ends with the arrival of the passenger or the freight at the final destination. Again, the aircraft themselves are subject to maintenance and turn-round schedules geared to the airline timetable. Airport workers live and travel from points outside the airport and form another important sub-system. The main goal of both planner and airport operator is to meet all these requirements, first to find the right sites, and then to ensure efficient operation.

Some aspects have recognizably geographical patterns, for example the movement of passengers through the system, which involves problems of airport access as well as the distribution of traffic onto the airline networks. Apart from such matters there are also micro-geographical problems within the airport complex, for example the movement of passengers from the airport car park through the terminal to the aircraft. Such movements can be very important, for they must relate to parallel movements of baggage and freight, quite apart from the need to ensure that passenger and aircraft meet at the right place and time.

At present it is not possible to discuss all parts of this system with equal facility; it is, for example, difficult to assess many of the environmental aspects. Here we shall pursue a limited number of problems, chiefly concerned with the all-important movement of passengers, and then deal with some environmental and site planning factors.

Airport traffic

A complete study of this area should cover not only the demand for air services, for both passengers and freight, but also the supply of aircraft and airport capacity to move the traffic generated. The results of such an analysis will also provide inputs to related problems of aircraft fleet procurement and ultimately must affect the aircraft manufacturing industry. More immediately, the capacity required will affect, and be affected by, aircraft turn-round and maintenance cycles.

Only a more catholic treatment is possible here. Since aircraft are predominantly passenger carriers no analysis of cargo operations will be given. Readers interested in this field are referred to the extensive work of P. S. Smith (1974). For related problems of aircraft demand and procurement the analysis by Ellison and Stafford (1974) may be consulted.

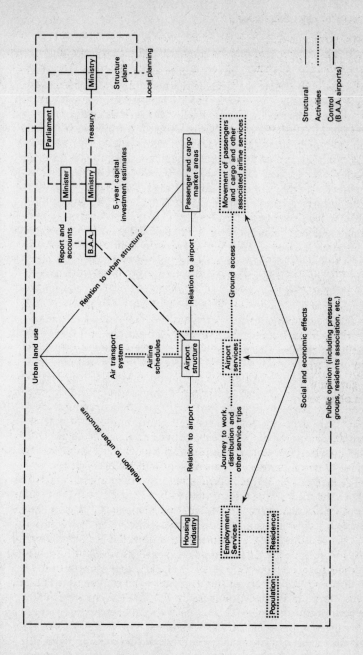

Fig. 1 The airport system

Analysis of demand

Air traffic forecasting is of primary concern since it is required for analyses of passenger access to the airport, and this in turn will affect the choice of an airport site. The distribution of traffic forms a basis for the determination of airport capacity required—not only how much, but also when the need will arise. Finally, the distribution of traffic will affect the Air Traffic Control system. We need to know the origin and destination of traffic within the airport's catchment and the pattern of traffic from the airport to overseas destinations. Airports, as far as the passenger is concerned, are not 'terminals', but nodes on two networks. More obviously they are part of an air route system, but they gather traffic by surface transport from the catchment area. Because of the particular characteristics of fixed-wing aircraft, air services can cover medium and long-hauls in excess of 250 km. and are often international in character. Surface access to the airport is by contrast a short-haul system and one which connects all airports within the country. Most effort has gone into forecasting traffic by air, and it is only relatively recently that demand from the local catchment area has been studied in detail. For broad brush studies of air traffic it is possible to consider demand as homogeneous and to estimate inter-city, and hence inter-airport flows, but for most purposes demand must be broken down into separate categories. Thus we identify both business and non-business passengers who may be residents of the home country, or come from overseas, giving four possible groups. In turn, passengers may travel on scheduled services, by charter services or on business-owned or private aircraft. For large airports, the first two categories, i.e. commercial aviation, are the prime concern, and less attention is paid to general aviation represented by business executive, private and club aircraft. For smaller airports, general aviation becomes a much more important issue and may indeed represent the majority of traffic movement.

The methods employed depend upon the availability of data and the scale of the study. What was possible with the resources of the Commission on the Third London Airport, Roskill Commission (1971), may not be possible for smaller regional studies. Much data may be derived from other planning studies, e.g. population forecasts, but such data may not always be sufficiently detailed for airport analysis which uses sophisticated methods. In fact data have to be sought from a large number of sources, a reflection of the airport's position in a complex community. Thus, the recent 'Northern Region Airport Study' (1974) lists nine local authorities, five government departments, six airlines, five tour operators, quite apart from other sources in industry and elsewhere. For whatever method is ultimately used, and particularly for those employing time series, it is necessary to ensure that spatial units are comparable. Boundary differences or changes are more common than might be supposed.

Early studies relied on trend analysis. Horonjeff (1962) compares the historical growth of a city's airport traffic with that for the country as a whole. The resulting ratio may be adjusted for differential trends, e.g. population growth for the city as compared with the national trend. Finally, the adjusted ratio may be applied to national estimates for the future year for which a forecast is required. Observations of trends in air traffic growth led to speculation as to whether the upward slanting curve approximated a constant rate of increase, i.e. was exponential, or was in fact a logistic curve that would eventually level off. Such time series analyses assume that past trends are an indicator of the future, and this applies to later, more refined, studies based upon regression analysis. The use of the latter arose from observations that air traffic is dependent upon certain economic variables, for instance incomes or fare levels, whose influence may be reflected in the elasticity of demand, i.e. price and income elasticities.

Bjorkman (1964) gives an excellent account of this approach. He not only includes economic variables such as price, fare structure, and income level, but also recognises other factors such as travel time, or geographical differences in market types. Basically, traffic is expressed as a function of the chosen independent variables. By studying previous development, where all factors are known, the coefficients in the model may be estimated by including a representative number of cases. The validity of the derived model may then be tested statistically. Thus in additive form, the basic model is given as follows:

$$T = E_a . X_a + E_b . X_b + \ldots + E_i . X_i + C$$

Where T = Traffic
E = Elasticity
X = Independent variable
C = Constant

In logarithmic form the coefficients show the relative effect of a variation in each factor, i.e.

$$\log T = E_a . \log X_a + E_b \log X_b \ldots + E_i \log X_i + C$$

Based upon a realization of the importance of economic variables such as price, fare structure, income level, and travel time, and their influence upon elasticity, Bjorkman constructed a family of econometric models based on regression analysis. He noted the limitations of this type of model, in particular the purpose of travel, whether for business or tourism, the stage of market development and the geographical differences between travel potential between one region and another, which may all affect the rate of elasticity. Differences in education, commercial and political development and other historical reasons are also quoted.

For the U.S.A. at any rate, greater insight into travel habits resulted from Lansing & Blood's study of the travel market in that country (Lansing & Blood 1964). The influence of such factors as age, family composition, and educational levels were investigated as well as economic elements such as disposable incomes and occupations. From such empirical evidence it became possible to calculate the 'propensity to fly' on both business and non-business trips. The use of travel speeds in Bjorkman's formulations leads on to questions of travel time, and considerable work has been done on the value of travelling time—a more refined measure.

The calculation of propensity to fly was attempted in this country by the research team of the Commission on the Third London Airport (1970). The basis of the calculation was an Air Passenger Survey at Heathrow and Gatwick which included data on incomes, age, family composition, and occupation. Both British and overseas passengers were included. Although place of residence was included in the questionnaire, the calculations on propensity to fly distinguished only between British business and non-business passengers, giving a 'national' figure. Very little can be said about regional differences that may be present.

The distribution of the traffic, both from catchment to airport and for inter-airport flows, is most often handled by cross-sectional analysis using a gravity model. Even for air transport the literature on the use of such models is large and will not be duplicated here, except to note characteristics that affect air transport. In an early application D'Arcy Harvey (1951) substituted the volume of air traffic for the interactance being measured. Of greater interest, he supplemented the mass factor by the addition of a component 'a' which he termed a 'community of interest' factor, i.e.

$$T_{ij} = k. \, a. \, Q_i^{b^1} \, Q_j^{b^2} \, / \, D_{ij}^{b^3}$$

where T_{ij} = Traffic flow between points i and j
a = community of interest factor, measured, e.g. by the incidence of telephone calls between i and j
$Q_i \, Q_j$ = population of cities i and j
D = distance between i and j
k = constant
$b^1 \, b^2 \, b^3$ = parameters to be measured

The use of a general population figure as a mass factor, and the use of distance for D, is often too crude to give adequate explanation, and subsequent applications have usually substituted the volume of traffic for population in the numerator. A moment's thought will also suggest that the traveller is more concerned with the time and cost it takes to travel rather than the distance. Hence distance is now expanded to include these two elements to form a 'friction' or 'deterrent' measurement. Even when distance is used, various exponents have been recorded according to area and route with a variation of 0·5 to 3·0.

It is possible to speculate both within and away from the framework of the gravity model, which with its derivatives, is essentially a practical tool. Wilson (1969) showed that the probability of the distribution of a traffic flow occurring is proportional to the number of states of the system which would give rise to that distribution, subject to any constraints on the model. Using a probability maximizing principle he was able to show that the most probable distribution is the same as the gravity model formulation. In other words, given the total number of trip origins and destinations for each zone for some homogeneous person trip purpose, the costs of travelling between the pairs of zones, and some total expenditure on transport in the region for the point of time chosen, then there is a most probable trip distribution pattern between the zones. This distribution is represented by the gravity model. Whether or not one accepts the respectability of the model, its various progeny have proved useful tools in traffic forecasting.

Speculating away from this model we could ask the basic question of whether air travel was the only mode of travel that satisfied the travel need we are concerned to study (Quandt and Baumol 1966). Abstract mode models start from the journey characteristics, and then consider the relative merits of particular modes. Hence modes of travel can be categorized by key elements which will affect their attractiveness for particular journeys. The general form of a simple abstract mode model could be in terms of the cost, trip time and frequency of service between two points i and j. A particular mode's chances would then be:

$$T_{ijk} = f[P_i P_j . C.H.F.]$$

Where T_{ijk} = traffic flow for mode k
$P_i P_j$ = population of two points i and j
C = cost ⎫
H = trip time ⎬ for modes
F = service frequency ⎭
If there are n modes serving i and j, then e.g.

$$H = g[H_{iji} \ldots H_{ijn}]$$

For each mode separately,

$$T_{ijk} = f_k [P_i P_j . C.H.F.]$$

Howrey (1969), taking Cleveland airport figures covering the thirty most used routes serving that airport, set out to compare the predictive accuracy of abstract mode models with that of gravity models. His basic conclusion was that it was difficult to improve upon the prediction of a simple gravity model, while the predictive accuracy of abstract mode models was sensitive to the form of the model used. Of the five forms explored, four were rejected on the basis of significant differences in the parameter estimates for two of the years taken. The survivor of the group produced forecasts inferior to those of the several gravity model formulations used. Even so he noted substantial errors in all cases: a plea for the continued experimentation in this field.

So far we have considered techniques for forecasting inter-airport flows, and while airport planners need to know the proportions of traffic on each route system, there is the more particular need to concentrate upon getting the traffic to the airport. Similar techniques have a place here too, since we are measuring similar flows at an earlier stage, but on a different scale. Geographically we are talking about the airport's catchment area, its definition, and potential. Here the question of accessibility is very important and often cannot be left to a measurement of airline distance, or even road or rail distance.

Surface access and demand

By way of introduction we should perhaps remind ourselves of the importance of accessibility in air transport. The customer is interested in total journey time from door to door. Hence accessibility enters at all stages of his journey, which we can visualize thus:

1. Journey to the airport
2. Movement through the airport
3. Airport to airport journey
4. Movement through the destination airport
5. Journey to destination

In the case of (3) there may be one stage or multiple stages involving changes of aircraft.

The models discussed so far have been applied to (3) but for airport studies (1) and (2) are more important. Stages (4) and (5) are the points where complementary airport studies might be expected to join up with our own particular study. They rarely do since we take the airport as the system and not the traveller. We are confronted then by (1) and (2) as lying within our orbit.

Parry Lewis (1971) has pointed out that there is a prima facie case for supposing that the ratio of those who actually fly to those who might be expected to fly if access to the airport was of no consequence will be positively correlated with accessibility, i.e.

actual passengers/expected passengers $= \alpha + \beta$ [accessibility] $+ \epsilon$

where ϵ is a small randomly distributed error of zero mean. Airport accessibility will then affect the propensity to fly, i.e. the generation of traffic. Strictly we should say the propensity to fly from a particular airport for a given travel purpose. If there is a choice of airports, then we are led on to a consideration of relative accessibility.

Following our observation that the journey to the airport is only part of the total journey, it follows that the ratio of airport journey to total journey time will depend upon the duration of the air journey. On short hauls, for example London to Paris, surface access may account for up to 50 per cent of the total, whereas on longer hauls it may drop to 8–10 per cent. Again the time to process through the airport may become critical on a short-haul journey—an aspect rarely considered by geographers. Time is more important than distance, and a glance at the cost-benefit analysis of the Roskill Commission (1971) reveals the importance of user costs. The latter includes not only the running costs for the use of a car, or rail and bus fares, but also a time cost. The latter is the opportunity cost of the time spent travelling and makes the assumption that such time has a cost. Since the time might otherwise be spent working or in leisure activities, most attempts to cost working time use income as a basic measure, either with or without allowances for the empty desk left behind. For leisure time the position is more uncertain and some proportion of the working time figure is taken. This is not the place to embark on a lengthy discussion, but for air transport the work of the Roskill Commission (1971) may be consulted, while Gronau (1970) discusses various ways of approaching the problem. We should note that there will be differences between time costs for business and for leisure travel. The extent to which a detailed analysis incorporating all the foregoing elements is carried out depends upon the scale of the study being undertaken. What is necessary for the study of London's major airports, undertaken with extensive financial backing, is not possible for the study of a small regional airport. However, the problems of the latter may serve as an introduction.

Biggin Hill, best known as a wartime fighter airfield, was taken over for civil use in 1959 and its later prospects as a general aviation airport for South London was the subject of studies carried out by a group of consultants of which the author was a member (Stratford 1967, 1972). The function of this airport is to serve business executive, club, and private flying: what is called 'general aviation'. Access to the airport is only possible by road, either by car or a country bus service. Preliminary demand surveys suggested that travel costs were less important than club and flying instruction fees for many recreational flyers, while business aviation was more cost and time-sensitive. Travel time in particular was important, most obviously when air taxis were hired to facilitate urgent business appointments. In common with many small airfields, part of the airport revenue came from rented industrial land, chiefly for small aviation-oriented firms, of which there were six at Biggin Hill in 1967. Their locational requirements are not under discussion here but for most of them good access was essential. A road time survey was carried out using road time data from the Road Research Laboratory and with sample runs at peak and off-peak times. Isochrones were drawn for each ten-minute interval from the airport and were repeated for adjacent airports with similar facilities—in this instance White Waltham and West Malling. Points of equal travel time to each pair of airports were plotted as 'time indifference' lines, and these defined the overall catchment of Biggin Hill as lying between the fifty-minute and one-hour contours. Survey results showed a marked fall-off in demand beyond the thirty-minute isochrone, with very little traffic beyond the fifty-minute mark. For the purpose of the study, the catchment for more intensive demand analysis was taken as the area within the fifty-minute isochrone, which included most of South London. Use of estimated time for the road system in 1980 increased the envelope, but account had to be taken of neighbouring airports which would bring Biggin Hill's catchment to the thirty-minute isochrone. Within the catchment, club and private demand showed no marked fall-off with distance/time: demand seems to depend more upon the number of 'enthusiasts per acre' within the South London catchment area. The ultimate time penalties which enthusiasts are willing to endure are large, judging by the number of boat owners who undertake three-hour journeys or longer to the south coast from London on a summer week-end.

Business interests are more closely defined by time/cost relationships and are more akin to commercial airline demand. There are special elements. Since many business aircraft are used for day-return trips, a thirty-minute access time to Biggin Hill allows five hours contact time on a total journey of 300 miles for a ten-hour day. The fastest alternative gives only 1·5 to 2·0 hours. This type of trip is most significant when destinations lie off the main airline routes, and it applies to domestic as well as international travel. The ability to make contacts with a minimum expenditure of time lies at the root of most business executive aviation, and the larger the spatial system within which the firm operates, the more this is true. It may also enable contacts to be made that would not otherwise be considered. Lack of congestion on the roads and at the airport are further important time elements .

A development of this approach was undertaken for the Northern Airports Study (Stratford 1974). In this study three airports are involved, with the possibility of new sites replacing or augmenting them. Taking just the two major airports at Newcastle and Teesside, isochrones were again calculated and the time indifference line between the two determined (Fig. 2). This line was then modified to take into account the effects of congestion by measuring peak and off-peak times. Thus under peak-time conditions the indifference line shifts three miles northwards. Business travellers tend to use scheduled air services at peak times, while tourist traffic occurs more frequently at off-peak periods. The indifference line defining the catchments was adjusted to the ratio of business and tourist travel demand expected, a calculation that reduced the shift to approximately 1·5 miles. Further adjustment was then made to take into account the lower air cost of travel from the airport nearer the destination. The resulting envelopes then formed the basis for establishing the zones from which traffic would arise. The proportion of traffic going from a zone to a given airport was then based on the ratio of the sum of the surface access cost, together with the difference in air cost between airports. Given the forecast of passenger traffic from each airport and the proportion of traffic from each zone to each airport, the number of passengers using each airport can be expressed as follows:

$$X_{iN} = P_{iN} \cdot N_i / N_N \cdot F_{Ny}$$

where X_{iN} = Number of passengers using Newcastle airport from zone i
P_{iN} = Percentage of total passengers using Newcastle from i
N_i = population of zone i
N_N = total population of catchment
$(\sum_i N_i P_{iN})$
F_{Ny} = forecast number of terminal passenger movements for year y using Newcastle airport.

Total number of passengers for Newcastle is $\sum_i X_{iN}$

As a final essay in this field, we may briefly consider the problem faced by the Roskill Commission with respect to the Third London Airport. Their terms of reference were to consider the timing and need for a third airport and possible sites for it. The question of access and

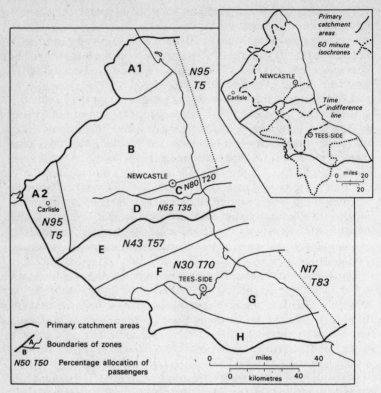

Fig. 2 Regional airport catchment areas (Newcastle-Teesside) Inset shows original
        time indifference line and its adjustment to give primary catchment division
        (Stratford and Associates 1974)

demand for air services from each possible airport or combination of
airports is particularly acute. Firstly, the problem is oriented towards a
London aiport, but the existing airports at Heathrow and Gatwick dom-
inate the whole country as far as international services are concerned.
Their catchment is national rather than regional, and hence all other airports in the country capable of providing such services are alternatives.
In fact only Manchester was included in the four systems of airports
analysed, and even this catholic choice brought its own data problems.
Two related points will be discussed here to demonstrate the difficulties
of the task; a full account may be found in the Commission's Report
(1971), the Papers and Proceedings Stage III (1970) and in the paper by
Carruthers and Dale (1971).

Two different surveys were used for the surface access demand model.
The earlier one conducted by the Government Social Survey for 1968
covered four London airports (Heathrow, Gatwick, Luton and Southend),
Manchester and Southampton. In this survey passengers were asked for
the origin and destination of their trip. The later survey conducted for
the Commission in 1969 covered Heathrow and Gatwick and asked
passengers for their area of residence rather than trip origin. Estimates
of actual passengers were made from the 1968 survey, while estimates
of the propensity to fly for leisure purposes, and hence an estimate of
expected traffic, were made from the evidence of the 1969 survey. Wide
variations in the ratio of actual versus expected passengers were found,
which the Commission suggested were due to the fact that different
airports had been covered in the two surveys, and that origin had been
asked for in 1968 and place of residence in the later 1969 survey. The
variation was greatest for areas adjacent to the airports. In a subsequent
regression analysis to investigate the possible correlation between the
ratio of actual versus expected passengers and accessibility, differences
in the areas covered and in zonal boundaries used in the two surveys
seem to have been ignored, and the results are suspect.

Parry Lewis (1971) considered that the discrepancies resulted from
the peculiar piece of geographical behaviourism that results from the
question 'where did you begin your trip to the airport?'. Thus, a passenger
from Glasgow who stayed overnight in London before continuing his
journey to Heathrow might well give London as the origin of his journey
to the airport. Asked for his place of residence, as in the 1969 survey, he
would give Glasgow as his answer. In any comparison between actual
and expected traffic the use of the two surveys would produce an over-
emphasis on the London area, and an underweighting of areas outside
the South East. From what can be gleaned of the analysis, the spatial
data employed were not homogeneous, and the results must be suspect.
The consequences of using such data in regression analysis have been
discussed by many authors, but here the paper by Poole and O'Farrell
(1971) seems most appropriate. Parry Lewis also criticized the use of
an average accessibility index in the regression analysis, and argued that
total accessibility produced more plausible results.

More practically, the accessibility constraint used reflected badly on
the remote site at Foulness, which with its higher user costs, made it an
unlikely choice. For this reason the criticisms levelled against the Commission's management of the access problems are important for any
future work, more particularly the extent to which remoteness and the
cost of access can actively discourage air journeys.

Airport terminal movement

The final link in the chain from the point of origin to the aircraft is the movement that takes place between the passenger's arrival at the airport and boarding the aircraft itself. This terminal 'interface' where transition from surface to air takes place may also be considered a bridge between the demand for air services, represented by the passenger, and the airport and airline capacity required to serve it. In practice this is not quite true since some processing can occur at city terminals. We are concerned with the space/time implications of terminal throughput; a micro-geographical problem that has implications for terminal design.

Earlier we noted that, from the passenger's viewpoint, total journey time was the key variable, and the relative importance of any stage in the journey depends upon the total journey time. For short-haul journeys time spent on the ground can be critical, and we usually think in terms of improving surface access to the airport. Careful time path analysis of movement through the terminal can demonstrate other bottlenecks. Table 1 (Sealy 1970) plots a time path for a short-haul route through the Heathrow terminal. The figures make little allowance for delays and they also assume that the passenger arrived and checked-in at close-out time for the flight. For the most critical path on the London-Paris route with an eighty minute elapsed time, the journey to the airport represents 38 per cent of the total, and airport processing 46 per cent of the total. A delay in movement through the airport of thirty minutes, or an early arrival, would reduce access time to 27 per cent and processing would increase to 61 per cent of the total. This simple example demonstrates the importance of terminal handling and suggests why 'shuttle' operations of the kind recently introduced by British Airways on the Glasgow service can produce significant savings in total time. However, there may be more than one path to be considered; a good example is the processing of baggage through the terminal. The use of Critical Path analysis can show where time savings would be most worthwhile. Such analyses are employed by airport and airline authorities not only to gauge the efficiency of passenger or baggage movements, but also to evaluate the turn-round cycle of aircraft arriving and departing from the airport.

Airport capacity

So far we have discussed the evaluation of passenger demand and its related spatial problems of access. To complete the study, the other half of the system covering the supply of capacity to meet the demand should be studied. This is an operational problem concerned with two aspects of capacity, the provision of adequate runways, and terminal capacity.

TABLE 1

Sample time path for passenger movements from point of origin to departing aircraft[1]

London–Paris (Pier stand aircraft)
Heathrow airport 1969

Event	Elapsed time (minutes)
Journey to airport	30
Park car	38
Check-in concourse	43
Check-in	50
Immigration	53
Departure lounge wait	57
Pier gate	60
Board aircraft	67
Engine start and push-out	80
Customs–2% of occasions, add 15 mins.	95

[1] Passenger has hand-baggage only, arrives at airport by car, arriving and checking in at close-out time for flight.
Source: Sealy, Institution of Civil Engineers (1970).

Until recently, most studies took runway capacity as the key measure, but the advent of wide-body jet airliners such as the Boeing 747 or the Lockheed Tristar has enabled a larger number of passengers to be handled for the same number of aircraft movements. Thus, aircraft movements have tended to rise at a slower rate than passenger numbers, making terminal capacity more critical. As far as London's airports are concerned, terminal capacity was first seen as the important issue in the Civil Aviation Authority (C.A.A.) report (C.A.A., 1973). This document sets out the major steps in calculating aircraft movements needed to handle the demand over various route lengths and the runway and terminal capacity required. A summary of the findings is given in Table 2 taken from this report.

Environmental effects

The airports of the 1930s created few environmental problems and could be absorbed within their regions with little difficulty. Even after 1945 little noise was heard, except for what one might call a grumbling groundswell, around the very largest airports like Heathrow. With the advent of the jet airliner after 1958 the situation became more serious since the jet made much more noise. Traffic expanded steadily through the 1960s and with it came environmental disturbances. The degree of disturbance depends once again on the size and type of airport, with the major airports like Heathrow posing the most critical problems.

TABLE 2

Forecast capacity at Heathrow airport (percentage excess (+) or deficiency (−) of capacity)

	Heathrow operation	Runway Capacity		Ground area Capacity	
		1980	1985	1980	1985
No Channel Tunnel	Mixed	+14	+12	+ 9	−12
	segregated	+ 9	+ 8		
With MK I Channel Tunnel	Mixed	+18	+16	+14	− 5
	segregated	+13	+11		

Notes i) 1985 figures include 1 runway at Maplin, and assume Luton closed.
     ii) Mixed operation—take-offs/landings on both runways.
     iii) Segregated operation—take-offs on 1 runway, landings on the other.
     iv) Central traffic forecast figures used in calculation.
Source: C.A.A. (1973).

We may define the environmental effects as those influences upon the surrounding area that result from the operation of the airport. Broadly, we may distinguish two categories (Sealy 1967):

1. Direct effects—safety, restrictions affecting land use, noise, pollution, employment in aviation activities and contributory airport services.

2. Indirect effects—secondary employment, including the multiplier effect. Long-term effects on land use planning, including the possibility of growth pole effects.

Both economic and social influences may be detected in this list, while the impact of the various items may extend over a long-term period. Indeed, to cover adequately this aspect of airport development would require a separate volume and some selection has to be made here. Noise is chosen because it is an example of a social problem and it provides a contrast to the earlier discussions in this chapter. Also, although much has been written about noise, there is little in the geographical literature on the subject. However, Table 3 gives an idea of the equally fascinating problems of employment that arise, and interested readers should consult the references given in the section on Further Reading (p. 28). The place of environmental studies is also suggested in Fig. 1.

The problem of noise

The definition and measurement of noise is simply explained by Waters in the book by Stratford (1974), while the original work on the Noise and Number Index (NNI) may be found in the Report of the Committee on the Problem of Noise (1963) under the chairmanship of

Sir Alan Wilson (Wilson Committee), and a sequel in a second survey
(Office of Population and Surveys, 1971).

The geographer might be forgiven for taking the 'best available' index
as his starting point, but he would be advised to make sure of its limitations. Unlike some effects upon our environment, noise can be measured

TABLE 3
Environmental effects of airports on employment

*a) Port of New York studies for proposed New York airport Morris County site.
Estimates 1980*

Regional level

	Number of employees	
Primary on-site	28 300	
off-site	11 000	
		39 300
Multiplier effect of primary	55 830	
Local business employment—sales to visitors, hotels, etc.	23 050	
Employment from industries supplying airport needs	16 400	
Secondary industry attracted	N/A	
		134 580
At 2·5 persons per family, Total population resulting from above		336 450

Local level

Primary and multiplier	47 465	
Remainder not estimated		
Population represented by above	118 600	
Estimates of secondary employment generated in local area range 10 000–70 000. At lower figure this gives local population total		143 662

Source: P.N.Y.A. (1960).

b) Balance sheet of employment impacts. Heathrow 1969–70

	Factories		Offices	
	Firms	Employt.	Firms	Employt.
Effect on location decisions:				
i. Positive impact	50	1500	43	5000
ii. Negative impact	124	12 000	0	0
Effect on location evaluation:				
iii. Positive impact (benefits)	220	23 000	83	12 000
iv. Negative impact (dis-benefits)	340	36 000	79	12 000

Source: After A. G. Hoare (unpublished Ph.D. thesis, Cambridge University).

as pressure vibrations. We can define noise as 'unwanted sound', but this poses the question, unwanted by whom? As Waters points out, what is sweet music for some is an unpleasant noise for others. Again, does the same noise affect people living in different environments in the same way? Noise measurement has gone some way along this path, whereby the simple measurement in decibels (dB) has been modified to take account of human susceptibilities.

Modifications of the basic measurement take account of human susceptibility to higher frequencies (dBA), to the intensity of sound at particular frequencies (PNdB), duration and pure tone (EPNdB), and the number of aircraft heard (NNI). The NNI developed by the Wilson Committee (1963) is the unit used for planning purposes in the United Kingdom. It is not an international unit, and other countries use variations, see for example Stratford (1975).

The control of noise nuisance may be tackled under two headings:

1. Control at source by building quieter aircraft.

2. Indirect control. This includes increasing the distance between source and recipient, silencing equipment, control of land-use development, and noise abatement procedures for aircraft movements.

Both involve government legislation to define limits. Two aspects will be considered to demonstrate the problems involved, firstly the use of Minimum Noise Routes (MNRs), and secondly the regional impact of noise.

Minimum noise routes

Airport noise restrictions use the PNdB scale, and for Heathrow the limits are 110 PNdB for day and 102 PNdB for night operations. Noise monitoring units are situated four to six miles from the take-off point, as shown in Fig. 3. Only the inner area is monitored, and there are currently only five monitors so that evasion is possible by tracking clear of these points. The question of take-off paths leads us to the possibility of MNRs, and the official case, following a report by the Noise Advisory Council (NAC) in 1971, is that traffic should be concentrated along MNRs rather than dispersed.

Hart (1972) has criticized the use of MNRs. Apart from reservations on the need to separate flight tracks by $45°$ for safety reasons, he considered the shortcomings of the NNI as important. Briefly, he sees the index as being inadequate for the following reasons:

1. The data used is now out of date (survey year was 1961).

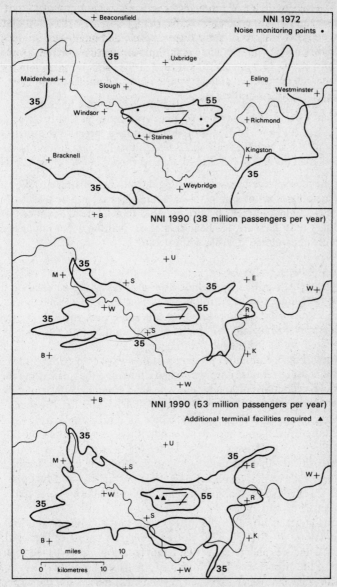

Fig. 3 Heathrow noise contours 1972 and 1990 (after C.A.A. 1973)

2. The measurement of annoyance was based on averages and no estimates of dispersion about the average were made. Using multiple regression analysis of annoyance on noise and number of aircraft, McKennell (1965) obtained a multiple correlation coefficient of only $R = 0.20$; i.e. only 20 per cent of the variation in annoyance between people is explained by the noise and number of aircraft.

3. The threshold value of 80 PNdB might have been applicable to Heathrow in 1961, but not to other areas, or even Heathrow at a later date. Thus the NNI is used to indicate a threat to the environment at a threshold value of 35 NNI, but if the background noise is less than 80 PNdB, the threshold value should be 30 or even 25 NNI.

Hart has some remedies, such as using the number of aircraft taking off as a measure of number in place of 'aircraft heard', and he tries tentatively to devise a method that obviates the need to measure annoyance directly. The fact that there are deficiencies suggests that the wider implications of noise control may also show shortcomings.

Regional impact of noise

All airport studies now include a noise survey which is based on the plotting of noise contours around the airport for 35 NNI and above. From a knowledge of aircraft movements and routes, the distribution of flights over time, and the type of aircraft used, noise plots may be calculated producing the familiar lobate patterns around the airport, as shown in Fig. 3. Computer programmes now exist to produce suites of contours using various runway configurations, and they can allow for the noise reductions of quieter aircraft. Most planning authorities use the contours as a basis for land-use restrictions within the affected areas.

Some authorities have recently shown misgivings concerning the NNI and noise control—the best documented is the study by the Councils of East Sussex, West Sussex and Surrey for the Gatwick area in 1971. There is also evidence that the density of population in the noise-affected area around Heathrow has increased since 1961. Within the 50 NNI zone seven boroughs showed an increase in population above 10 per cent between 1961 and 1968.

Finally, let us turn to some further aspects of annoyance and background noise. Richards (1970) plotted the public's noise ratings against the NNI and was able to show that annoyance was not confined to areas close to the airport. For Heathrow his formula suggested that areas of considerable annoyance extended beyond eight miles from the airport. Later (1971) he developed a disbenefit/benefit ratio (D/B) where D was the number of people seriously affected as shown by his formula, and

B was an estimated total number of aircraft passengers per annum. Hart (1972) criticized this procedure as being too crude in that measuring the number of people affected was only part of the exercise concerned with evaluating annoyance.

In his work Richards was aware of the limitations of the NNI with respect to background noise, and he limited his formula to 'urban areas'. Background noise is part of a much wider question of area noise levels. We do not possess 'noise surface' maps, except for small areas, and most of these do not include rural areas. This seems to demand micro-studies of sample environments, both urban and rural, but to progress in this direction we must consider other fields of study. Pilot work carried out for land use—transportation studies cover some aspects, for example London Traffic Survey, Vol. III (1969), or the Kingston-upon-Hull plan (Freeman, Fox and Associates 1972)—considers road noise levels with respect to varying environments. This type of investigation has also been undertaken in the U.S.A. As a sample, a study of Philadelphia (Bragdon 1971) considered environmental effects, including noise, for two areas in Delaware County. The approach was a synthesis of noise recordings from 25 locations, together with opinion surveys around each station. The survey included indoor and outdoor background noise, and the vertical effects of tall buildings. Interestingly enough, noise diminution in the far field closely approximated the inverse square law, unless disturbed by reflections from buildings. The survey found noise to be the major disbenefit, with aircraft noise from the adjacent airport as the main source (followed by children playing—as far as residential areas were concerned!). Statistical analysis of the data series revealed some interesting areas for further research, for example Chi-square tests suggested a correlation between a person's awareness of environmental problems and his perception of noise intensity.

For airports in more rural areas background noise levels are lower, but we have little to go on here. In any case, rural areas include recreational facilities and cannot blandly be taken as convenient noise sinks for passing aircraft. As a tailpiece, Bryan (1973) suggests that one-fifth of the population are more sensitive to noise than planners assume, while another third are not bothered at all. Manifestly we have still a lot to learn about the impact of noise.

Physical siting of airports

We began this chapter with an enumeration of the factors affecting airport location and we may conclude it by considering some of the physical aspects of site selection. Whereas other elements in the airport system may react to the changing needs of the airport, the actual site can only be abandoned at a heavy price. Given sufficient space, expansion is possible, as is contraction, should this alternative prove necessary. The site must, then, be suited to the forecast size and purpose of the airport and at the same time cause the least disturbance to the surrounding neighbourhood. The approach to the problem involves a familiar constraint; what can be done depends upon the size and type of airport under consideration. The urgency for a military airfield is very different from the ten-year deliberations for a Third London Airport.

One can arrive at a possible location by studying other airport requirements; for example preliminary demand forecasts outline the main catchment, but such detailed forecasts need an accessibility measurement for particular sets of points. One possible starting point is to work out the accessibility surface for the catchment with respect to surface transport. This approach was tried by Armstrong and the author for the area of the South Hampshire Airports Study (Armstrong 1972), using graph theory. The analysis was taken in stages, moving from a connectivity matrix of one/zero form to a matrix weighted for road times and 'air user' population located on the network. For the latter, a 156-node network, links were weighted according to the road travel time for that link, using values derived from Road Research Laboratory data regarding road speeds and link length. In addition a further weighting for air user population was attempted. This entailed establishing 'catchment areas' for each link, i.e. all points within the catchment are closer to that link in time than any other. Watersheds were therefore points equidistant from two links, rather than two nodes, as is more usual. The assumption is that people will travel directly to and from the links using the major roads (A and B roads in this instance), and will use minor roads only as feeders. Allocating the air users to this mesh of catchments entailed severe data problems, for to do the job properly we need to know the socio-economic factors affecting the propensity to fly, for the enumeration districts (ED's) of the area. Moreover, if both business and leisure trips are to be covered, two sets of data are required. Values of the 'propensity to fly' for business purposes were derived from the Roskill Commission data, together with occupation group data from the 1966 Census. The estimates that resulted were at the urban and rural district level, and were then scaled to ED level using existing population distributions for the cells. A similar procedure was used for leisure trips, which together with the business estimates, formed the total air-user weighting. The final ED figures were then transferred to the link catchments. However, there was still an uneven distribution of population within the link catchments. To overcome this, each link was taken as two directed links (i.e. i to j, and j to i), and weighting for possible movements in each direction could then be achieved

Powering the weighted connectivity matrix to its solution time, and summing the matrices, yields accessibility values for each node to the rest of the region weighted for travel time and population. In the time available it was not possible to complete the powering process to solution time, and the process was stopped at the C^{15} matrix. Previous experience with powered matrices of this order showed a tendency for patterns to stabilize between five and ten iterations, so the fact that solution time was not reached was not as critical as might be supposed. Node values were then plotted and the accessibility contours drawn in, giving the final map illustrated in Fig. 4. In this map column sums (terminals) are plotted, but it is equally possible to draw row sums (origins) if required. Since the map is drawn from a weighted matrix, high accessibility is indicated by high values.

From the map, areas of search for new sites can be made, and these confirm evidence from other sources that the Romsey area was the most promising one in which to conduct such a search. Subsequent analysis follows the pattern given for the methods now to be considered.

For the study of sites for a Third London Airport a different approach was employed, to narrow the choice from a wide initial catchment based on a one-hour isochrone from central London. Some extension beyond this limit was made to include areas well served by road and rail, giving an area that extended from Wolverhampton and Grantham in the north, to Bournemouth in the west (see Fig. 2 Appendix 5 of the Report of the Roskill Commission, op. cit. 1971). Within this catchment the site search was made independently by the author and the Ministry of Housing and Local Government. Further constraints were made by a sieve process, for example land within thirty miles of Heathrow was eliminated, chiefly on air traffic control criteria, as well as land within five miles of continuously built-up areas. Physical suitability for the remaining area was defined by six alternative airport layouts with varying runway systems. Runways were taken as 14 000 feet in length, and runway separation as 2500 feet, giving, with the terminal, a total area of approximately 14 square miles. Within the airport site, the maximum acceptable relief was taken as 200 feet, and the maximum tolerable variation of runways as ±35° from a 045/225° orientation. Gradient analysis of the area within these constraints was made at a scale of one inch to the mile which eliminated totally unsuitable zones. Further analyses at 1:25 000°scale, and by field investigation, produced a final list of 48 sample sites. In conjunction with the Ministry results and a subsequent search by the Ministry using less stringent constraints, the final 'long list' of 78 sites was produced.

Further refinement, involving for instance cost analyses for defence costs, noise, and air traffic control, together with any constraints caused

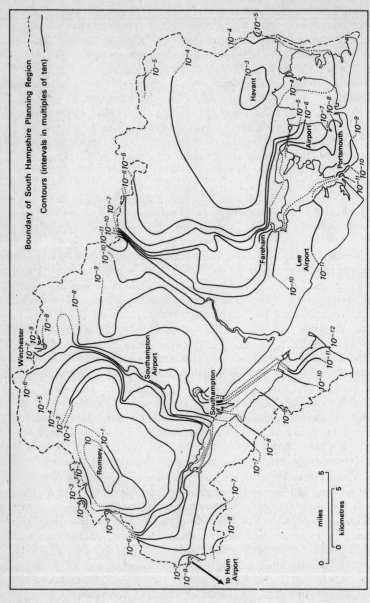

Fig. 4 Road accessibiligy surface for South Hampshire Planning Region (After H. W. Armstrong 1972).

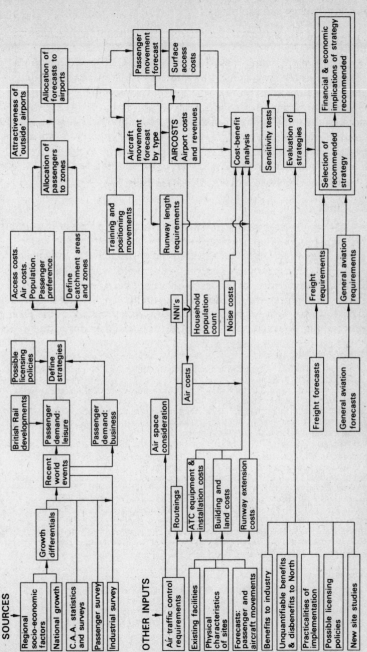

Fig. 5 Northern Region Airport Study: methodology diagram (Stratford and Associates 1974).

by planning requirements, finally reduced the list to the four sites eventually chosen.

Recent regional airport studies have made use of such inputs for a computer search programme. The difficulty is the measurement of gradient, and here the work of the British Geomorphological Research Group (Brown and Crofts 1973, Gardner and Rhind 1974) in delineating slope gradients has a direct application, not only for single sites, but also for strategic planning of airports throughout the country. It will also be evident that work concerned with background noise as previously discussed would likewise improve the input for site searches. Even so, for final sites, local surveys would seem to continue to be necessary.

Conclusion

The need to analyse spatial data enters at many points of the airport planning process. Here we have considered passenger demand and accessibility of airports, one aspect of the environmental problem and some requirements for site selection. Other fields, such as cargo traffic, and other environmental influences, have not been covered, but also merit geographical investigation and require the application of techniques from both physical and human geography. As a summary of the planning process, Fig. 5 outlines a working plan for a regional airport study.

Further reading

Alcaly, R. E. (1967) 'Aggregation and gravity models; some empirical evidence', *Jnl. Reg. Sci.*, 7, 61.
Barnard, J. K. & Oyen, D. B. (1971) 'Transport nodes and local service airports', *Jnl. of Trans. Econs. and Pol.*, 5, 120.
Board of Trade (1966) *Aircraft noise (Report of International Conference)*, London.
Brown, S. L. & Watkins, W. S. (1968) 'The demand for air travel', *Record 102, Highways Research Board*, Washington D.C.
Dawson, L. G. & Sills, T. D. (1972) 'An end to aircraft noise?' *Aeronaut. Jnl.*, 76, 28(
Federal Aviation Administration, (1965) *Planning the airport industrial park*, Advisory Circular AC 150/5070—3, Washington D.C.
Filani, M. O. (1973) 'Air Traffic forecasting: an input-output technique approach', *Reg. Studies*, 7, 331.
I.C.A.O. (1970) *Aircraft noise in the vicinity of aerodromes*, doc. 8857.
Johnston, R. J. (1973) 'On frictions of distance and regression coefficients', *Area*, 5,
Lilley, G. M. (1974) 'Noise—future targets', *Aeronaut. Jnl.* 78, 459.
Lloyd, P. (1972) 'The aeroplane as a threat to the environment', *Aeronaut. Jnl.* 76, 5
Royal Aeronautical Society, (1971) 'Symposium on airports and transport aircraft', *Aeronaut. Jnl.*, 75, 529.

References

Armstrong, H. W. (1972) 'A network analysis of airport accessibility in South Hampshire', *Jnl. of Trans. Econs. and Pol.*, 6, 1.
Bragdon, M. (1971) *Noise Pollution: the unquiet crisis*, Philadelphia.
Bjorkman, Bo. (1964) *Demand elasticity in air transport*, Institut du Transport Aérien, Paris.

Brown, E. H. and Crofts, R. S. (1973) 'First geomorphological map of Britain',
  Geog. Mag., **46**, 137.
Bryan, M. (1973) 'Noise laws don't protect the sensitive', *New Society,* 738.
Carruthers, R. C. and Dale, H. M. (1971) 'The modelling of surface trips to the
  Third London Airport', *Reg. Studies*, **5**, 185.
Civil Aviation Authority, (1973) *Forecasts of air traffic and capacity at airports in
  the London area,* London.
Commission on the Third London Airport (Roskill Commission) (1970) *Papers and
  Proceedings,* Stage III, Vols. VII and VIII.
– (1971) Report, London.
Committee on the problem of noise, (Wilson Committee) (1963) *Noise,* London.
Ellison, A. P. and Stafford, E. M. (1974) *The Dynamics of the Civil Aviation
  industry,* London.
Freeman, Fox and Partners, (1969) *The London Traffic Survey,* 3, London.
– (1972), *Kingston-upon-Hull and nearby areas: Land-use transportation study*, London.
Gardner, V. and Rhind, D. W. (1974) 'The creation of slope maps by a photo-
  mechanical technique', *Area,* 8, 14.
Gronau, R. (1970) 'The value of time in passenger transportation: the demand for
  air travel', *National Bureau of Economic Research, Occasional Papers,* **109**, New York.
Hart, P. E. (1972) 'Population densities and optimal aircraft flight paths', *Discussion
  Papers in Economics,* 37, University of Reading.
Harvey, D'Arcy, (1951) 'Airline passenger traffic; pattern within the United States',
  Jnl. of Air Law & Commerce, 18, 157.
Horonjeff, R. (1962) *The Planning and Design of Airports,* New York and London.
Howrey, E. H. (1969) 'On the choice of forecasting models for air travel', *Jnl. of
  Reg. Sci.,* 9, 215.
Lansing, J. R. and Blood, D. M. (1964) *The changing travel market,* Survey Research
  Centre, University of Michigan, Ann Arbor.
London Traffic Survey, *see* Freeman, Fox and Partners (1969).
McKennell, A. C. (1965) *Aircraft noise annoyance around London airport,* SS 37,
  Central Office of Information, London.
Noise Advisory Council (1971) *Aircraft Noise: Flight routeing near airports,* London.
Office of Population and Surveys, (1971) *Second Survey of aircraft noise annoyance
  around London,* Social Survey Division, London.
Parry Lewis, R. (1971) 'Mis-used techniques in planning: the forecasts of Roskill',
  Reg. Studies, 5, 145.
Poole, M. A. and O'Farrell, P. N. (1971) 'The assumptions of the linear regression
  model', *Trans. Inst. Brit. Geogr.,* 52, 145.
Quandt, R. E. and Baumol, W. (1966) 'The demand for abstract transport models;
  theory and measurement', *Jnl. Reg. Sci.,* 6, 13.
Richards, E. J. (1970) *Noise and the design of airports, in World Airports, the Way
  Ahead,* Institution of Civil Engineers, London.
– (1971) 'Noise and Society', *Jnl. of the Royal Soc. of Arts,* **129**, 678.
Roskill Commission, *see* Commission on the Third London Airport.
Sealy, K. R. (1967) 'The siting and development of British Airports', *Geog. Jnl.,*
  133, 148.
– (1970) *Integration of Air and Surface transport, in World Airports, the Way
  Ahead,* Institution of Civil Engineers, London.
Smith, P. S. (1974) *Air Freight. Operations, marketing and Economics,* London.
Stratford, A. H. (1975) *Airports and the environment,* London.
Stratford and Associates, (1967) *The future of Biggin Hill as a Civil Airport,*
  Maidenhead.
– (1972) *Development Plan for Biggin Hill Airport,* Maidenhead.
– (1974) op. cit. Chap. 1.
Wilson, A. G. (1969) 'The use of entropy maximising models in theory of trip
  distribution, modal split, and route split', *Jnl. of Trans. Econs. and Pol.,* 3, 108.
Wilson Committee, *see* Committee on the problem of noise.

3 Airport strategy

In our previous discussions we have taken the airport as the unit, but found it necessary on occasion to refer to relationships with other airports in the country. The burden of this chapter is to widen the field to take account of a nation's airports as a whole, i.e. the strategic considerations of planning. This suggests the notion of a National Airport Plan as a vehicle for undertaking the task, which in turn raises issues of ownership and control.

Whatever system is envisaged there is a basic need for two data sets, one giving the distribution and characteristics of population and socio-economic development—from which air transport demand may be fore-cast—and the other providing information on airport capacity at all levels, and associated air service patterns. In both cases a knowledge of trends is required entailing time series for analysis. In the United Kingdom, using regional as well as national figures, some knowledge of a national air travel market may be approximated—backed up by data giving passenger composition and movements through the airports—but there is no single source of information. The position is even less satisfactory when it comes to air cargo prospects. Airport capacity and traffic is an easier task as far as existing services are concerned, and a summary may be found in Masefield's paper (1972), which also brings out the hierarchical pattern of airports. Not all airports will handle the same spectrum of traffic; the two ends of the scale will be the major international hubs, Heathrow for example, and the small general aviation and 'social service' airfields at the other.

There are several ways of categorizing airports. In setting out standards for operating practice, the International Civil Aviation Organization (I.C.A.O.) categorizes by length of runway, but sometimes the division is based on traffic. As an example, Masefield (1972) suggests seven cat-egories, using runways as the key element as follows:

Category 1. Major international, capable of handling the largest com-mercial aircraft on an all-the-year-round basis. Full customs, immigration and catering services.
At least two runways, one not less than 3750 m for take-off, the other not less than 2500 m for landing.

Category 2. As for (1), but with one runway not less than 3050 m.

Category 3. Medium and short-haul international and domestic services on a year-round basis. Similar to (2), but with a runway not less than 2550 m.

Category 4. Seasonal international charter and domestic scheduled services, with a runway not less than 2250 m.

Category 5. Occasional charter services, business and training operations with a runway of not less than 2000 m.

Category 6. Short charter and domestic services and all aspects of general aviation. Runway of 1600 m.

Category 7. General aviation and short take-off and landing (S.T.O.L.) aircraft, with a runway minimum of 1220 m.

The number of existing U.K. airports under each category of this scheme would then be:

Category 1 = 1
          2 = 2
          3 = 2
          4 = 5
          5 = 4
          6 = 19
          7 = 11

Even allowing for the fact that we would expect a greater number of airports in the smaller categories, the above distribution is still lopsided, with only one airport (Heathrow) in the first division, and only five in the first three divisions. Masefield discusses this distribution with respect to population and traffic growth, showing the need for the development of nine airports outside the London complex, to serve the needs of the seven major regions as follows:

Southern Scotland—Glasgow, Edinburgh, Prestwick
Northern and North West Regions—Manchester
South Midlands—Birmingham, Castle Donnington
North East—Newcastle
Severnside—Bristol or Cardiff
Southern England—Bournemouth or Southampton.

Smaller airports would serve the South West, Wales, and the Highlands and Islands of Scotland.

Other schemes follow this pattern with variations, but most make it clear that not all the planning regions can support the same level of airport services. However, it could be argued that, for instance Manchester airport cannot serve the very wide catchment suggested, and indeed, vigorous support for the development of a major regional airport in the Yorkshire-Humberside area has often been advocated.

It is possible to model various combinations of traffic and their distribution between alternative schemes of development. The model developed by METRA (Department of Trade 1974) used by the Civil Aviation Authority (C.A.A.) in its assessment of the Maplin project, studies the effects of diverting traffic from London to regional airports in terms of access time and cost, journey patterns, including flying time and costs, and hence assessed the extra capacity likely to be needed at regional airports if such shifts were made. Runs of the model were made to predict patterns of national usage for four possible combinations of London airports and twelve regional airports. Table 4 gives the results, the most striking aspect of which is that there would be very little difference in the hierarchy except for Birmingham and Bournemouth. Such models should also take into account the consequences of traffic allocation, including environmental effects. The work of the Roskill Commission provided some insight into the difficulties that arise; there is uncertainty concerning passenger reaction to particular problems of access. Would passengers be prepared to pay the cost of using more remote airports? The question of the value of travelling time is still uncertain, while the question of environmental issues is still more uncertain. Even if an efficient plan emerged which passed any cost-benefit evaluation, it does not follow that that plan would be carried out. Would Manchester Corporation in effect contemplate a substantial transfer of traffic to Liverpool's airport at Speke if this was an 'efficient' solution? There is also the question of uncompensated costs which should on any efficiency criterion be compensated by benefits. Environmental disbenefits from noise and other amenity losses are likely to be large and inadequately covered.

Alternative solutions to strategic planning

Having reviewed the background, it is now possible to consider ways of accomplishing an airport strategy. Two extreme cases define the field:

1. A national plan, or national planning process, which involves a major commitment by the central government to carry it out.

2. A *laissez-faire* approach with a minimum of government regulation.

Hybrids of these exist, such as planning for major airports only. There are also variations in such questions as ownership, since a national plan could also entail state ownership of all civil airports, but this is not essential, just as some public ownership is possible under a *laissez-faire* system.

TABLE 4

Passenger traffic allocations London airports, Channel Tunnel and other airports (millions of passengers)

	1973 (year ending 30 Sept.)	1990 Scenarios				
		4	1	2	3	3B*
London airports						
Heathrow	19·8	55·2	38·7	38·4	38·1	38·0
Gatwick	5·7	23·9	15·7	15·7	15·1	16·3
Stansted	0·2	2·8	–	15·8	3·9	3·9
Luton	3·2	2·4	–	8·3	3·0	2·6
Maplin	–	–	25·6	–	–	–
Total	28·9	84·2	80·1	78·9	60·1	60·8
Channel Tunnel	–	7·5	8·2	7·6	10·0	10·5
Other airports						
Bournemouth	0·4	1·4	3·1	4·6	14·6	5·1
Birmingham	1·1	2·9	3·8	4·7	10·4	6·9
East Midlands	0·5	1·1	1·3	1·3	1·5	11·7
Manchester	2·6	4·6	5·2	4·9	4·8	4·9
Liverpool	0·5	1·2	1·2	1·2	1·2	1·1
Blackpool	0·1	0·5	0·5	0·5	0·5	0·5
Leeds/Bradford	0·3	1·0	1·0	1·0	1·0	1·0
Teesside	0·2	0·3	0·3	0·3	0·3	0·3
Newcastle	0·8	0·8	0·8	0·8	0·8	0·8
Bristol	0·3	0·8	0·8	0·8	0·8	1·2
Glamorgan	0·3	0·4	0·4	0·4	0·4	0·4
Norwich	–	0·1	0·1	0·1	0·3	1·4
Total	6·9	15·1	18·6	20·6	36·6	35·4
Total	35·8	107	107	107	107	107

* When Bournemouth and Birmingham traffic is constrained
Source: 'Maplin, Review of Airport Project', H.M.S.O. (1974)

A national airports plan

The need for an overall national plan is based on a number of factors:

1. Airports require large areas of land and heavy capital investment. It is necessary to allocate scarce resources in an efficient and equitable manner, and since land allocated to an airport has implications for land use in its vicinity, planning on an overall scale is essential.

2. Operating costs are high and few airports show a profit on their operations. This was particularly true in the 1950s and 60s when, for example, the three Midland airports made a cumulative loss of £390 000

after meeting capital charges in 1966–67. Rationalization of airport capacity is then one possible solution. Again, the quality of service offered is affected by too many airports fighting for the traffic, resulting in low frequencies and poor revenue returns. Co-ordination of airport and airline services should be efficiently administered, and this too suggests central direction.

3. Where surveys, and subsequent investment based on these, are carried out at a local level, there is usually little appreciation of the far-reaching effects of this action on neighbouring areas. For example, traffic catchments may overlap local boundaries, so that the action of one airport authority affects the others. For similar reasons, public enquiries into land use changes are also inadequate where many airport projects are concerned. The Stansted inquiry was perhaps the best example of this.

Planning structures set up to achieve national as well as local goals vary considerably with respect to ownership, control, and regulation. The theme and variations may be summarized as follows:

1. A national plan drawn up by central government for the complete ownership and control of all airports where civil air transport is carried out. Such plans do not usually include small general aviation airfields, with the exception of those which provide a service for isolated communities, and which would not be justified on purely economic criteria.

This is the extreme model and is more characteristic of centrally planned economies than those of western countries. The 1947 Plan for U.K. airports (Fig. 6) came close to this pattern, except that ownership was restricted to airports serving scheduled services. However, in view of the dominance of such services at this time, the exceptions were not as numerous as might be imagined.

2. National planning that does not envisage the establishment of a single master plan, but aims to control development according to need. Under these schemes ownership may be divorced from control, i.e. major airports may be owned by central government agencies, while control of the remainder may be exercized by regulation, including financial assistance.

The advantage of a single plan is that implementation is easier. However, there are severe limitations. Any single plan demands a knowledge of airport systems that we do not yet possess. Discussions in the House of Commons concerning future airport planning produced statements such as 'the solution of the problem requires a full systems analysis', but just how such an analysis might be accomplished was not so clear. The limitations of the Roskill Commission's work which dealt with four existing and seventy-eight possible sites is an indicator of the task of dealing with a national total of some sixty existing airports, together with an unknown number of possible new ones. Furthermore, the time scale of such a study would almost certainly render any subsequent plan redundant before it was implemented.

As a result of the rigidity of the extreme case, most planning falls into our second category, where the problem is looked upon as an on-going process, and where the approach to ownership and control is more flexible. It is possible for 'paper planning' to be undertaken centrally to provide a frame of reference for the development of a system of airports under mixed ownership. The Edwards Committee (Committee of Inquiry into Civil Air Transport 1969) put it in a nutshell: 'Preparing paper plans is one thing; having the power to implement them is another' (para. 903, p. 223) and again, 'Nothing we saw in the actual operation of airports suggested that central ownership of them all was necessary for efficient operation' (para. 905, p. 223) and 'It seems to us desirable to fit the ownership and management of airports to their function. This might be termed the principle of "control by the interested community" ', (para. 907, p. 223).

An alternative approach

The difficulties inherent in estimating future national and regional airport requirements prompt the suggestion that the industry should be free to find its own level of growth through market forces; those who require the services should pay for them. Whitbread (1971) contrasted a 'rigid plan' model with a 'competitive pricing model'. He is careful to note that his models are the two extremes, and he does not consider more flexible variants. However, his competitive pricing model is a good example of how this approach might operate.

Although not essential to the argument, it is assumed for the purpose of the model that ownership of airport capital is removed from public to private hands, i.e. the ultimate in decentralization. One further proviso is that compensation for nuisance is paid by those responsible for its creation, and as far as possible, paid to the losers. Airport corporations then become like classical firms faced with expenditures to be recouped by charging for the use of facilities. Compared with current systems of airport charges, this model would almost certainly lead to price discrimination between types of traffic, and between services at peak and off-peak periods.

Owing to the high proportion of capital costs it could be argued that competition would not prevail, since many would-be operators would not be able to finance development without aid of some kind. Hence

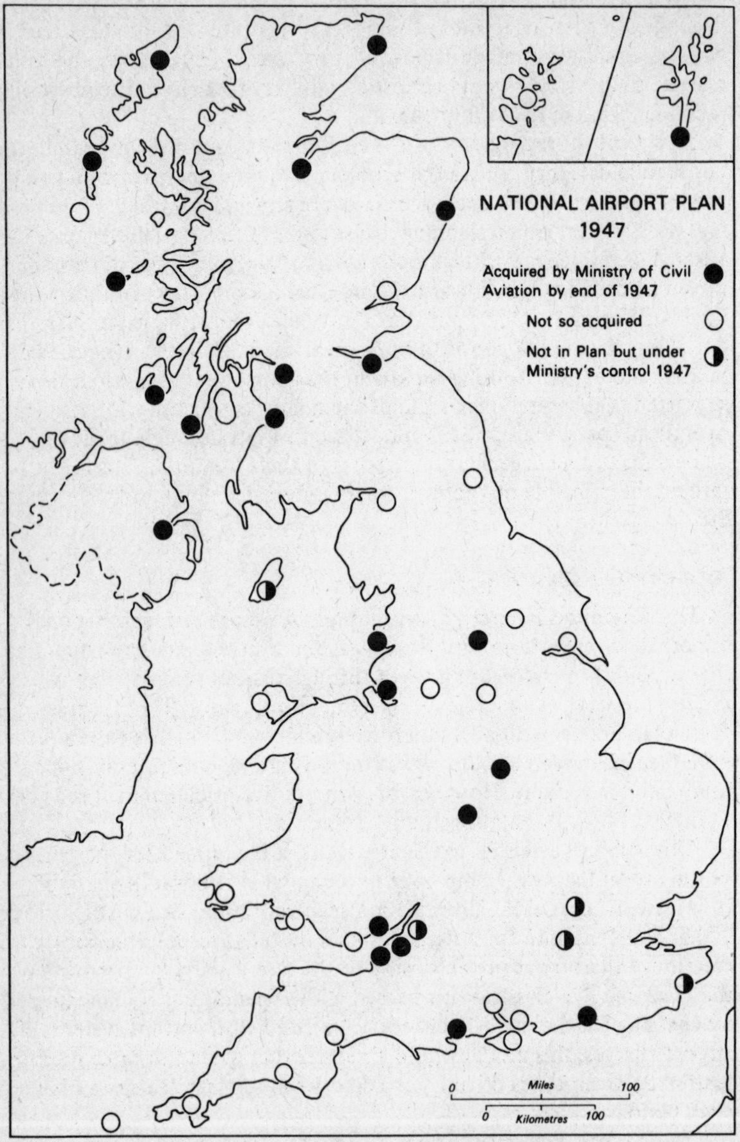

NATIONAL AIRPORT PLAN
1947

Acquired by Ministry of Civil
Aviation by end of 1947 ●

Not so acquired ○

Not in Plan but under ◑
Ministry's control 1947

Fig. 6a British Airports 1947 (Sealy 1967).

Fig. 6b British Airports 1975. (After Sealy 1967)

monopoly or some form of oligopoly would result, and one would be faced with a system less under control than other possible organizations. On the other hand, it could be argued that local competition from cities in close proximity, each aspiring to run local airports, could lead to unco-ordinated effort and too much competition. Whitbread sees no real evidence that either possibility need be harmful. Monopoly powers might be constrained by the possibility of entry by others, or by government regulation. The competitive situation only becomes wasteful of resources if expectations are seriously out of line with realization of revenue.

Efficient resource allocation might then be expected so far, but it is required that all significant spillover costs resulting from environmental nuisance should be internalized into the airport operator's costs. Here, as in any other system, there is the familiar problem of assessment and compensation. Various twists and turns are suggested. Thus, except in limited instances, the law at present does not allow compensation for nuisance by flying activities, and this leads to opposition to uncompensated, noisy projects such as airports. For this model we need to find out how much compensation the victims would accept to endure the nuisance, or else to move out. If the idea of 'amenity rights' (Mishan 1969) i.e. a legal right to a peaceful environment, could be defined, then Whitbread suggests airport operators could negotiate to buy out such rights. He admits that high transaction costs and the legal difficulties probably make this a non-starter. Similar difficulties arise with any notion of a 'compensation code' devised and controlled by the government, although generous compensation could restrain projects which produced 'too much nuisance'. Compensation for those not directly affected, for example those suffering from noise during outside recreation in wider geographical localities, is more difficult still, and the use of traditional land-use planning methods of prohibiting deleterious development is a blanket solution that may be applicable to National Parks but not to the less well-defined and scattered localities likely to be encountered here.

The competitive price model could conceivably approach an efficient allocation of resources; it has a built-in system for assessing consumer benefits, thus providing services where the demand exists. Furthermore, continuous assessment of benefits is allowed for, and economic incentives exist for decision-making. The biggest problem concerns external effects, particularly noise and amenity losses. Its success would depend upon an efficient method of compensation, and for the latter to be internalized within the operator's cost structure. For major airports where profitable operation is possible, the model has some merit, but for 'social service' airports serving isolated communities the model seems to be inadequate. Furthermore, the establishment of legal codes, operating regulations, the definition and control of compensation codes, as well as possible government regulation to restrict monopoly practices, entail a considerable field of government participation.

Conclusion

No single system has a monopoly of advantages. Both the extreme forms of rigid plan and competitive pricing models have severe disadvantages. Some element of planning is required—more particularly in the assessment of national and regional needs undertaken by bodies from both levels of government. Ownership is another question altogether, and a mixture of public and private ownership need not undermine an orderly approach to development; it could well ensure that local as well as national needs were met.

Further reading

Doganis, R. S. (1966) 'Airport planning and administration', *Pol. Quart.,* 37, 416.
Pegrum, D. F. (1973) *Transportation, economics and public policy,* 3rd edn., Homewood, Illinois.
Sealy, K. R. (1969) 'Air transport facilities and regional planning', *Aeronaut. Jnl.,* 73, 581.

References

Committee of Inquiry into Civil Air Transport (Edwards Committee) (1969), *British Air Transport in the Seventies,* Cmd. 4018.
Department of Trade (1974) *Maplin. Review of airport project,* London.
Masefield, Sir Peter (1972) 'An airports system for United Kingdom air services', *Aeronaut. Jnl.,* 76, 275.
Mishan, E. J. (1969) *The cost of Economic Growth,* Harmondsworth.
Whitbread, M. (1971) 'A framework for the efficient production of airport services', *Reg. Studies,* 5, 121.

4 British airport planning and strategy

The early period

The siting of British airfields is largely due to the two World Wars, for in both these the threat from continental Europe led to a clustering of sites in the eastern half of the country, and around the major cities. In the inter-war years grass airfields, which intruded little on the surrounding area, were dominant. Some, like London's Croydon airport, were former military sites, but others such as Speke airport at Liverpool, were new developments. Most civil airports were either privately or municipally owned, for the typical 200–400-acre sites costing up to £400 000, were within the financial capabilities of such bodies. Except for London, there was little co-ordination, and many of our present closely-spaced airports date from this period.

World War II saw the development of the heavy bomber which, with its greater wing loading, demanded concrete runways and more sophisticated flying aids. Thus the later military bases were a tempting legacy for post-war civil use, and indeed, apart from Lydd, no new site has been developed *ab initio* since 1945. The Labour government of 1945 put forward its National Airports Plan in the White Paper of that year. It included plans for the public ownership of airlines as well as airports, the former resulting in the three air corporations of B.E.A., B.O.A.C., and B.S.A.A. The airport plan was close to the 'rigid plan' model of the previous chapter, and was justified on the grounds of the enormous amount of public money that had been spent, or would be spent, in the future. In the event, the plan was somewhat nebulous, and did not emerge until 1947. Some forty sites were listed (Fig. 6) excluding London. Many were rather anomalous, for example Lancashire and Yorkshire were to have four airports, the Midlands two closely-spaced airports but East Anglia none at all. As time went on, development was concentrated upon those airports used by the airline corporations, including those for B.E.A.s ambitious domestic network.

The break came in 1950 when the Ministry agreed that Manchester Corporation should retain ownership of Ringway airport. Other airports followed the trend of municipalization that culminated in the White Paper (1961) which marked the final reversal of the 1945 policy of state ownership. Under the 1949 Civil Aviation Act, the Ministry retained statutory powers over airport development, and the abandonment of

any planning was not a necessary result of decentralization. Thus airports
for public use had to be licensed, while Ministry approval for new sites
was required, particularly if compulsory purchase orders were involved.
Financial assistance needed the sanction of both the Ministry of Housing
and Local Government and the Ministry of Aviation. In practice these
controls were liberally interpreted, and the incentive for development
came from the air corporations, private airlines, and local authorities.
The exception to this drift was London, whose airports deserve separate
treatment at a later stage.

Decade of conflict, 1961–71

Hindsight suggests that the title for this decade is appropriate in that
not only did it include the decentralization heralded by the White Paper
of 1961, but it also saw the establishment of the first airport corporation—
the British Airports Authority (B.A.A.) which brought together a group
of airports crucial to the national interest. The fact that three of them
were London airports is a measure of London's continuing domination
of air transport in Britain. The period also felt the impact of the modern
jet airliner, which not only demanded more airport concrete, but also
provided a quantum jump in working capacity over its earlier piston-
engined forbears. Even here there was uncertainty as to whether turbojet
or turboprop applications were suited to particular types of network.
Finally, the events leading to the battle for London's third airport
provided the incentive for more rigorous research into traffic and its
origins, and to a re-appraisal of the need for a more co-ordinated strategy
regarding airports as a whole.

In 1961 the newly-elected Conservative government stated that
although planning in the formative years after the War had been necessary,
the time had now come to relinquish such control. Most airports should
be run as business enterprizes, with government responsibility extending
to en route and other technical services. By 1961 only twenty-two airports —
remained under Ministry of Aviation ownership and control, including
the three London airports at Heathrow, Gatwick, and Stansted. There
were twenty-five municipal airports, and forty-eight private airports
with public service licences. The treatment of the state airports provides
an insight into the philosophy of the period. The international airports,
i.e. the three London airports at Heathrow, Gatwick and Stansted, with
Prestwick in Scotland, were the country's principal gateways, and were
to be placed under a public corporation—the British Airports Authority
(B.A.A.)—which took over control on 1 April 1966. A second group of
seven regional airports—Aberdeen, Belfast, Blackpool, Bournemouth,
Cardiff, Edinburgh and Glasgow—were to become the responsibility of

their local authorities, but the government accepted that financial assistance would be required to relieve the pressure on local ratepayers. Such assistance, it was emphasised, was only to be given where the 'aerodrome in question is regarded as one of a limited number indispensable to the national transport system' (White Paper 1961). Four had been taken over by local authorities by 1968, and the fifth, Edinburgh, was to come under the aegis of the B.A.A. The nine airports of the Highlands and Islands of Scotland, essential for the welfare of these areas, would continue to be subsidized and managed as a unit—for the moment at least—under the Board of Trade.

The White Paper (1961) had recommended the setting-up of a corporation to own and manage the major international airports, and the inauguration of the British Airports Authority in 1966 was the last major change in this period. The Select Committee on Estimates, in its report published in June 1961, had also recommended such a corporation, and in its evidence to this Committee, B.E.A. considered that 'an airport is potentially a keenly commercial undertaking and for this reason should be run on competitive business lines. A civil service approach is very often quite inappropriate'. It was hoped that the new corporation would co-ordinate the development of the four airports and deal 'in a more flexible, adaptable and rapid manner with essentially commercial problems and situations'. It is also important to note that the enabling legislation (Airports Authority Act, 1965) empowered the Corporation to 'provide or assume the management of any aerodrome in Great Britain' after obtaining the consent of the President of the Board of Trade. Edinburgh (Turnhouse) airport was the first airport, other than the original four, to be taken over in 1971. What was not made clear was the policy concerning take-overs, i.e. would the B.A.A. eventually assume the ownership of Aberdeen airport, since the local authority had no plans to do so? The case for doing so would presumably be that it was an airport indispensable to the national system, and could not be left in limbo.

The Board of Trade was involved in airport development in other ways too. It owned airports, it was responsible for negotiating international traffic rights, and provided navigational facilities. In relation to non-state-owned airports it had statutory and some non-statutory responsibilities. The former included making grants and giving consent to local authorities with respect to the development of airports, dealing with loan sanctions from the planning standpoint, and making regulations with regard to airport charges. Non-statutory responsibilities included navigational services, and the provision for planning and technical advice. It was also the confirming authority for compulsory purchase orders under the Town and Country Planning Acts.

At the regional level there were other complexities. The newly-established Regional Economic Planning Councils were given responsibility for airports and air services in their regions, and several made recommendations regarding airports in their planning reports. They existed alongside the six 'advisory committees for aviation' whose function was to advise the Air Transport Licensing Board (A.T.L.B.) on matters affecting air services within their area. Such committees covered Scotland, Wales, N. Ireland, the North, the North West, and the West Midlands. Their boundaries of jurisdiction overlapped those of regional planning authorities and did not in any case cover the whole country, as the list makes plain.

To summarize the trends of this decade is difficult, but it does seem to demonstrate that neither a rigid plan nor complete decentralization offer a solution. The contrast lies between the 1947 Plan on the one hand, and the intentions of the 1961 White Paper on the other. To some people this decade appeared to be a chaotic one with no underlying strategy, and this led to pleas for a return to more closely defined planning (Sealy 1965, Doganis 1967). There were certainly anomalies, both geographically, and financially. East Anglia, Wales and the South West lacked regional airports; East Anglia had no scheduled service airport, while in the South West three small airports at Exeter, Newquay, and Plymouth competed for the limited flights available. In South Hampshire too, three airports competed for traffic. Up to 1965 Bournemouth (Hurn) was the only one with a concrete runway and it handled 200 000 passengers a year. The development of Southampton (Eastleigh) resulted in the transfer of many services to that airport so that by 1967, Hurn's traffic had dropped to 20 000 passengers, and Eastleigh's had increased to 284 000. The South Hampshire Airport Study (Stratford and Associates 1970) has since recommended the development of Hurn as the regional airport. In the Midlands a radius of thirty miles took in three airports at Coventry, Birmingham (Elmdon) and the East Midlands (Castle Donnington). In the North, Manchester (Ringway) and Liverpool (Speke) stood cheek by jowl, while on the other side of the Pennines, Leeds-Bradford (Yeadon) battled with Teesside and Newcastle (Woolsington). The result, financially, was that many of these airports operated at a loss. The report of the Edwards Committee (1969) gives us the best résumé of the situation for this period, and Table 5 summarizes their findings.

Nevertheless, a pattern was emerging. The B.A.A. had taken control of the London airports on the one hand, while increasing regional awareness of the airport problem led to studies which held some hope that regional anomalies would be resolved. Many of those in which the author took part provided not only much-needed data, but also facilitated some progress in the analytical techniques needed to solve the problems

TABLE 5

British airports—financial results—year ended 31 March 1968

Airports	Number of airports	Income	Expenditure	Surplus (Deficit) before tax
British Airports Authority		£(000s)	£(000s)	(£000s)
Heathrow	1	15 291	11 133	4158
Gatwick	1	1711	2248	(537)
Stansted	1	301	465	(164)
Prestwick	1	1862	1825	37
	4	19 165	15 671	3494
Board of Trade				
Group 2	4	1265	1492	(227)
Group 3	8	179	558	(379)
	12	1444	2050	(606)
Municipal				
Where Board of Trade provide Air Navigation Services	5	3914	4304	(390)
Including self-provided Air Navigation Services	13	2265	3269	(1004)
	18	6179	7573	(1394)
	34	26 788	25 294	1494

Source: Cmnd. 4018, H.M.S.O. (1969).

(Stratford and Associates 1968). The event which marked the end of this period emerged from the recommendations of the Edwards Committee (1969 op. cit.). Their report is a document that all students of the subject should read. Of its many recommendations, the following are the important ones for our purpose:

1. The Government should promulgate, by statutory instrument from time to time as necessary, clear statements of civil aviation policy, indicating the importance to be attached to the various objectives.

2. British civil aviation in the 1970s should include a public sector, a mixed sector, and a private sector.

3. The Government statements of policy should constitute the terms of reference of a new Civil Aviation Authority. This Authority would be responsible for the economic and safety regulatory functions at present dispersed between the A.T.L.B., the Board of Trade, and the Air

Registration Board. It should also be responsible for the civil side of the joint National Air Traffic Control Services, for operational research, for long-term airport planning and for the main work of traffic rights negotiation.

The Civil Aviation Authority (C.A.A.) was set up by the Civil Aviation Act of 1971 and took over from the Board of Trade and other bodies in April 1972.

The period since 1971

The establishment of a body able to co-ordinate the multifarious aspects of civil aviation meant that it would now be possible to rationalize the 'paper planning' to take account of national and regional interests. Following the Edwards Committee, ownership would be mixed and would include airports owned by the B.A.A. as well as municipal and private fields, i.e. a compromise between a rigid plan and decentralization. However, there is a proviso to be noted. Attempts to get a clear responsibility for airports written into the C.A.A.'s constitution were largely unsuccessful, and its jurisdiction is mainly advisory. What was achieved may be found in Clause 33 of the 1971 Act which states that the C.A.A. should consider what airports are required and should make recommendations to the Secretary of State on the matter (Civil Aviation Act, Chapter 75.II.33., 1971). In the ensuing policy guidance White Paper (1972), airports get two lines which repeat the substance of the Act.

Fortunately, the C.A.A. has given some indication that it intends to take seriously its role with respect to airports. In its report on airport planning (C.A.A. 1972), the Authority sets out its approach to the problem. The report points out the difficulties which arise with any attempt to produce an ideal network, and makes the point that any such exercise would not take the place of regional studies, although it might form a complementary frame of reference. It considered its first task was to complete a group of regional studies with the aid of local authorities and outside consultants. These studies would be complementary to those that had been made for the London area by the Roskill Commission and its successors.

Studies for central England, the northern region and Scotland have been completed, while further studies have still to be finished, for example Severnside and the South West. From the summary available on the Central England Study (*Flight International*, 27 June 1974), the consultants recommended an ideal solution whereby Blackpool, Leeds-Bradford, Liverpool, Manchester, East Midlands, and Birmingham airports would be closed, and two new sites in north Cheshire and the West Midlands would replace them. Their 'next best' solution envisages Manchester and Birmingham only as remaining. The first is a good example of an approach through the cost-benefit evaluation of a computer model, but it seems very unlikely that such a solution would be acceptable in the near future for the communities concerned. The Northern Airports Study (Stratford & Associates 1974) also recommends two airports for the northern region at Newcastle and Teesside, both of which exist. The possibility of a single site replacing these two was considered, but not recommended. The fact that this study did not include Humberside, which came under central England, brings out forcibly the shortcomings of the regional approach. The C.A.A. has the task of putting the bits together.

We are left, therefore, with the outlines of a contingency planning system, one in which a central body is expected to advise on national strategy and to assist in regional and other studies, but where ownership is divided between a national corporation (the B.A.A.), municipal bodies, and private interests. The actual airport system itself remains much as we left it in our previous section, except that the B.A.A. has added Aberdeen and Glasgow (Abbotsinch) to its list (Fig. 6); in other words, the B.A.A. now owns the major Scottish airports. Whether this is an augury for the future in other parts of the United Kingdom is a matter for speculation.

London's airports

For our purposes two periods may be considered, the earlier phases up to 1963, which will be treated very briefly, and the more critical period that follows the events of 1963.

The early stages, 1945–63

Aided in the initial period up to the mid-1950s by various ex-military airfields, Heathrow became the focus of London's airports after its take-over on 1 January 1946. Ignoring detail, two major issues need discussion as a backdrop to more recent events.

The first concerns Heathrow itself which, as conceived by the Report of the Advisory Panel (1946), was to become the most ambitious airport scheme yet seen in this country. Three phases of growth were envisaged. Stage One was the existing R.A.F. airfield temporarily modified for civil use, Stage Two saw the full development of the double parallel runway system and central terminal, while Stage Three covered a final extension north of the Bath Road. The second stage was completed six years late in 1955, but Stage Three was doomed to oblivion by its close proximity to built-up areas, and was perhaps the first victim of growing public resistance to noise and disruption. Although cost-benefit appraisal still lay in the future, one cannot help feeling that the dice were too heavily loaded for this stage to survive. Growing traffic showed up the inadequacy of the terminal area, while technical advance made runways covering a large number of wind directions unnecessary. The re-working of the terminal area and runway system to its present shape began with the report of the Millbourn Committee (1957). Heathrow was then one of the first airports to feel the winds of technological change and public resistance.

The second issue concerns the support Heathrow needed from other airports. Up to 1953, Heathrow was 'supported' by a motley collection of ex-military fields, and the pre-war airport at Gatwick. The White Paper (1953) first recognized the need for an adequate alternative airport for London, and chose Gatwick as the site. The progress of the latter towards that status is a fascinating essay in uncertainty, but it cannot detain us here. Suffice it to say that Gatwick only became a feasible alternative in the mid-1960s. Apart from Luton and Southend, which are municipal airports and beyond the official ken, the only remaining member of the original group of supporters was Stansted. This pawn was retained at public expense lest the Queen and her Rook should require assistance in the future!

In 1961 the White Paper on 'Civil Aerodromes and Navigational Services' recommended the establishment of a corporation to run the international airports. This body, the B.A.A., took over London's airports, previously owned by the Ministry of Civil Aviation. Interesting here is the part played by London's airports in this decision. For this link in the chain we need to look at the Select Committee on Estimates Report for 1961. They first made a close scrutiny of costs and revenues, noting the heavy investment on the one hand, and the financial performance of the Ministry airports on the other. Capital expenditure at Heathrow had reached £32 million by 1960, with another £18 750 000 earmarked for the period up to 1970. The balance of income and expenditure showed a loss of over £2 million for each of the years between 1957—60, and this despite increasing traffic. The Committee found there were shortcomings in the charging of landing fees, and that there was insufficient drive to raise income from other sources, e.g. concessions to caterers, and other services. The best that could be said was that Heathrow was almost breaking even, but the remainder were below the line.

Some of the financial troubles arose from indecision with respect to the use of resources. The Committee resolved that the position of Gatwick in the hierarchy ought to be made clear, and then, of course, there was Stansted. The Committee wanted a decision in the near future as to whether a third London airport was needed within the next fifteen years, and if so, whether Stansted was the best site. On the whole this was a timely and pertinent survey, but one is left wondering what would have happened if they had recommended a national airports authority. The Government, goaded by the Select Committee's report, and burgeoning traffic, appointed an Inter-Departmental Committee to study the need for a Third London Airport. This committee, appointed in 1961 and reporting in 1963, forms the starting point for the final phase of London's development.

From 1963 to the present day

The contined expansion of facilities at Heathrow and Gatwick marked this period, as it did the earlier phases. For example, at Gatwick £1·5 million extension to increase the capacity of the terminal and to extend the runway to 2500 m. was begun; a process that eventually led to still further terminal development and the extension of the runway to its present length of 3150 m. But the problem that dominated everything else was the question of a Third London Airport, sparked off by the Select Committee Report of 1961 and the subsequent Inter-Departmental Committee Report, CAP 199 (1964).

The philosophy of this report was based on the need to find a site that could become a large omni-directional airport equal in stature to Heathrow The degree to which the history of Gatwick affected the Committee's thinking is difficult to judge, but there is a little doubt that there was a desire not to have a repeat performance of this kind. The main criteria used were basic aviation needs; the size and nature of future traffic, the rate of handling this traffic at both current and projected airports and the Air Traffic Control requirements. In the summary to the report, we also find concern that the site should be no more than an hour's journey from central London and still be compatible with air route requirements. The conclusions embody two further observations. First, that the planning of the airport should be part of a comprehensive scheme embracing housing and industry, should take particular care to avoid noise problems, and that any new residential development for the area should be made compatible with the airport. Secondly, that the questions of when and where London should have a fourth airport should be taken up in about five years' time.

As is well known, the site finally chosen was Stansted. This airport had the disadvantage that it could not be operated with Heathrow to full capacity unless each airport was limited in the range of routes served, but the Committee noted that this would apply to all sites within at least 50 miles of central London. The use of Stansted would also reduce military flying and would require the development of high quality agricultural land. The Committee thought that these disadvantages were outweighed by the advantages, which apart from the needs of air transport, included good road access and suitability as an area for the development of the housing and other urban facilities that would be required.

Most of the main issues were, therefore, included in the report. The tragedy was that access, planning and noise were either hardly covered at all, or disposed of in brief paragraphs. Even the aeronautical data were open to question, and we are left in the dark over the sources and studies used in the report. Since compatibility with other planning issues was mentioned and the Committee included representation from both the Ministry of Housing and Local Government and the Ministry of Transport, it is hardly conceivable that such studies were not made.

The Public Inquiry into the proposed development of land at Stansted opened in Chelmsford in December 1965 and lasted until February 1966. The Inspector's report was submitted in May 1966 and the White Paper, 'The Third London Airport' (1967), setting out the Government's views followed.

The White Paper acknowledged the need for further study and claimed that in the year since the publication of the Inspector's report such a study had been carried out. Within the thirty pages of the Paper little evidence of the character of this study can be perceived. The contents page lists a section on the case for Stansted, but the opposing view can only be disentangled from a section on alternatives to Stansted; nowhere is there a good independent statement. A further study of the traffic at London's airports is given, updating the figures given in CAP 199 and including the eventual use of large aircraft such as the Boeing 747. It is difficult to see how the figures were obtained; for example growth rates for terminal passengers handled are on a scale ranging from 9 to 10 per cent per annum in 1968 to 5 per cent by 1980 on the 'lower limit' forecast, and from 13 per cent decreasing to 10 to 11 per cent per annum on the 'upper limit scale'. The 'most likely' forecast comes between the two. No indication is given of how the reduced rates were calculated, or the assumptions that lay behind them. On the basis of its traffic forecast, the Government expressed the view that the new airport would be needed by the mid-1970s, provided that both Heathrow and Gatwick could be fully utilized. If not, the need would arise in the early 1970s as originally suggested in CAP 199.

No clear statement of the shortcomings of Stansted was given in the study. A major point here is the impact of the airport on regional planning. This affects the issue in three ways: first, the relative growth of regions in the U.K. and their potential contribution to air traffic; second, the local planning effects of a new airport and third, the relationship of London to the other regions—a national planning problem. Commenting upon the Inspector's point that regional considerations deserved more discussion, the White Paper notes (p. 19) that 'In the Government's view the strongest of the objections to Stansted is on planning grounds'. But it was also the Government's view that 'the Inspector's argument that a third London airport would attract more economic activity in the South East is beside the point in the light of evidence in Section II of the White Paper of the need for a third London airport'. Having made this grand assertion it then becomes too easy to dispose of agriculture and green belts. No attempt was made anywhere to assess costs and benefits of one possibility against another, and this applies too to the summary dismissal of the Bedford and Silverstone sites. As far as the latter is concerned, the Paper noted that the strong point for this site was 'on the grounds of regional planning'. The implications of this Paper point irresistibly to the fact that the Government had virtually ignored both public evidence at the inquiry and the Inspector's report. Subsequent reaction to the White Paper was more intense than that raised by the original document, CAP 199. Indeed at this stage the whole question of the Third Airport became a political issue between the Government and the public. Many and varied were the arguments put forward; everybody became an airport expert (Stratford 1966, Brancker 1967, Noise Abatement Society 1967).

In January 1968 the Board of Trade, now responsible for civil aviation, put forward a plan to re-align the runway system at Stansted from the original 05/23 of the existing runway to 02/20, or nearly north-south. The completion of runways on this new axis would reduce noise nuisance in the area to $\frac{2}{3}$ of the number of people affected by the old alignment. The extra capital cost involved in this venture was estimated at £8 million for the first two runways and would include taking over an extra 700 acres over and above the 2800 acres already involved. Further development beyond 1980 would make a further pair of runways necessary and this, of course, would entail more land and another public inquiry. The Ministry of Housing and Local Government were to write to local authorities in the area asking for their comments on the new proposals.

The whole affair had come before the Council of Tribunals and its report in favour of a new inquiry came out only hours before the annoucement by Mr. Crosland to the House of Commons on Thursday, 22 February, that the Government had decided that a new inquiry into the siting of London's Third Airport would be held. Mr. Crosland noted that whereas the new runway alignment would reduce noise, the eventual need for more land to extend the system to a 'double parallel', four runway system, entailed the use of more land and was in fact virtually a new project. It is possible to believe that the Government changed its mind on a technical point, but Mr. Crosland's remarks are nearer the point, 'The Government have not taken this decision merely in response to the legitimate pressure brought to bear by members of this House, but because a clear sense, locally and nationally, has emerged that there is public anxiety, and debate about the decision. Six years after CAP 199, London's Third Airport project had ended up where it had started.

In May 1968 the Government set up a Commission on the Third London Airport under the chairmanship of Lord Roskill. The nature of the Commission is interesting in view of the shortcomings of the public inquiry in large scale matters such as airports, and the publication of the White Paper on 'Town and Country Planning' (Sealy 1967). The latter recognized that current inquiry procedures for problems which raise 'wide or novel' issues were inadequate and that there was a need for new procedures. However, it confined its conclusions to a promise that the Government would be 'examining whether or how such procedures can be changed for these exceptional cases'. The Roskill Commission may be taken, perhaps, as a bit of advanced notice of this thinking.

Announcing the new Commission, Mr. Crosland said, 'The form of the inquiry must meet two requirements. On the one hand, this is one of the most important investment and planning decisions which the nation must make in the next decade; this points to an expert, rigorous and systematic study of the many and complex problems involved. At the same time, the decision will profoundly affect the lives of thousands of people living near the chosen site; and this calls for an adequate method of representation of the local interests affected'. To try and satisfy both requirements the Commission would sit both as a Commission of Inquiry, sifting and assessing evidence, and as an Inquiry where interested parties could be represented by counsel and have the right to cross-examine, both at local inquiries into possible sites, and before the Commission itself. Some five stages were envisaged in the Commission's work, i.e.:

1. Evaluation of the whole range of possible sites.

2. Evidence of a local character concerning sites shortlisted in Stage 1.

3. Research into matters relevant to the choice between various sites; work that will be concurrent with Stages 1. and 2.

4. Consideration of Stage 3 results, including cross-examination of experts.

5. Counsels for interested parties may test and inquire into material produced at previous stages.

The work of the Commission was a landmark in airport planning, and is better known than the crucial events that preceded its formation. Reference to some of its methods has been made in Chapter 2, and our task here is to assess its place in a wider context.

The most important departure from previous practice was the decision to set up the Commission's own research team to investigate the major problems alongside studies from outside bodies. The team's analysis is reported in the Papers and Proceedings of the Commission, Vol. VII, while outside studies are the burden of Vol. VIII (1970). The attempt was made to assess questions of site, traffic, and the environmental effects, and to include all of them within a cost-benefit analysis. The evalution of benefit and disbenefit in cost terms brought much criticism, particularly with respect to environmental issues (Lichfield 1971). Indeed the dominance of passenger user costs in the final table, compared with noise and other amenity effects, brought the criticism that this was an economist's solution.

The final choice of Cublington as the site for the Third Airport over the less environmentally-damaging Foulness site reinforced the feeling that this had been a limited approach to the problem. On regional planning grounds there were also misgivings. Although the team were aware of the work of the South East Planning Team, the fact is that the South East Plan itself was not published until after the Commission had completed its work. In effect the argument is as old as aviation itself. For the operator and his customers, a site close to the market, and with good access to its various parts, is a prime need. On environmental grounds such sites incur the greatest disbenefit. For regional planning much depend upon whether remote sites, which are environmentally advantageous, are also compatible with other land-use developments. The question is whether the airport with its demands upon labour, housing and services will form a 'growth point' in the area, and if so, whether this is in accord with overall plans. For sites closer in, there is the reverse possibility of 'overheating' an already developed region where, for example the airport's demands for skilled labour will worsen an existing labour scarcity.

The Government accepted the Commission's recommendation that a Third London Airport was needed in April 1971, but having weighed with care the economic arguments identified by the Commission (Department of Trade, Review of Maplin Project 1974), it took the view that regional planning and environmental issues were of paramount importance, and that it was worth paying the price to develop the Foulness site. In 1973 the Maplin Development Authority (M.D.A.) was set up under the Maplin Development Act of 1973 to undertake the reclamation of land at Maplin Sands. The order to proceed required the permission of the Secretary of State, i.e. no reclamation until Parliament consented. Further, comprehensive appraisals of the project were to be carried out. On coming to office, the new Labour Government announced in March 1974 that it intended to re-appraise the whole affair, and that in the meantime no further work at Maplin would take place. Ten years after Stansted (or as some prefer it, £1 250 000 plus, later) London remained as it was.

The re-appraisal had to face the fact that events had not stood still. Operationally, the introduction of 'wide-body' jets had proceeded faster than had been forecast, meaning that the increase in traffic would be handled by fewer aircraft movements, and hence terminal rather than runway capacity would become more critical. Secondly, traffic at Gatwick in the 1970s revealed a spreading of the peak summer load into the 'shoulder' months of June and September, again making for more efficient use of airport space. The prospect of the construction of a Channel Tunnel would also imply some diversion of traffic from the airports, though the Tunnel project is not now to be proceeded with.

Revised traffic forecasts by the C.A.A. (1973) noted these trends and showed that capacity limitations at London's airports would not occur until 1980, and depending upon the impact of the Channel Tunnel, possibly not until 1985. Table 2, from the report, shows that terminal rather than runway capacity was the limiting factor. Given this situation, it now seemed possible that existing airports might be expanded to cope with the expected traffic, at least through the 1980s. The review of the Maplin Project (Department of Trade 1974) took these findings into account, together with further appraisals of environmental effects, and proposed four possible scenarios for the future. They were not intended to provide definitive answers, but to be illustrations of possible solutions. A summary of the four possibilities forms a fitting conclusion to the story; it remains to be seen which, if any of them, will provide a basis for more decisive planning proposals. A good deal will depend upon how effectively the disbenefits of aviation, especially noise, can be reduced in the next decade. Without such developments it is hard to see the harassed populations around Heathrow and Gatwick lightly accepting still further expansion of those airports.

The Scenarios

1. With Maplin. Heathrow and Gatwick would take additional traffic up to levels compatible with existing B.A.A. development plans. Gatwick would be limited to one terminal. Luton and Stansted would be closed, and Maplin would take traffic not accommodated elsewhere in the London area.

2. Without Maplin, but with substantial development at Luton and Stansted. Heathrow and Gatwick would develop as in (1), but with a deliberate policy of not necessarily providing all the capacity demanded. Passengers not accommodated would use regional airports or other modes, or would not travel at all.

3. Without Maplin. Regional diversion. Heathrow and Gatwick as in (1), and Luton and Stansted used at minimum viable levels. This scenario provides a way of exploring reduction in London demand by pricing

policy, or limitations by planning policy. A large proportion of even South East passengers would have to use regional airports.

4. Without Maplin. Major development of Heathrow and Gatwick. In this scenario, Heathrow and Gatwick would meet almost all London area demand. Heathrow would be extended westwards over the present Perry Oaks sludge disposal works, and Gatwick would require a second terminal. Remaining traffic would be split between Luton and Stansted.

Further reading

Abelson, P. W. & Flowerdew, A. D. J. (1972) 'Roskill's successful recommendation', *Jnl. Royal Stat. Soc.,* Series A (General), **135**, 467.
Adams, J. G. U. (1971) 'London's Third Airport', *Geog. Jnl.,* **137**, 468.
Department of Environment, (1972) *Maplin Airport, choice of site for runways.*
Fordham, R. C. (1970) 'Airport planning in the context of the Third London Airport', *Econ. Jnl.,* **80**.
Wilkinson, K. G. (1972) 'Air transport development between the United Kingdom and Europe in the next twenty years', *Aeronaut. Jnl.,* **76**, 343.
Zeigler, H. (1971) 'The major development trends in air transport and European co-operation', *Aeronaut. Jnl.,* **75**, 309.

References

Brancker, J. W. S. (1967) *The Stansted Black Book,* Stratford & Associates, Maidenhead
Civil Aviation Authority (1972) *Airport Planning. An approach on a national basis.*
– (1973) op. cit. Chap. 2.
Civil Air Publication 199 (1964) Report of the Interdepartmental Committee on the Third London Airport.
Doganis, R. S. (1967) A national airport plan, *Fabian Tract* 377, London.
Edwards Committee (1969) op. cit. Chap. 3, under Committee of Inquiry into Civil Air Transport.
Lichfield, N. (1971) 'Cost-benefit analysis in planning; a critique of the Roskill Commission', *Reg. Studies,* **5**, 157.
Noise Abatement Society (1967) *The Third London Airport,* London.
Roskill Commission (1971) op. cit. Chap. 2, Commission on the Third London Airport
Sealy, K. R. (1965) 'Towards a national airport plan', *New Society,* 9.
– (1967) 'Stansted and Airport Planning', *Geog. Jnl.,* **133**, 350.
Stratford & Associates (1966) *Studies of the site for a Third London Airport,* Published for the N.W. Essex and E. Herts. Preservation Assoc., Maidenhead.
– (1968) *Airport and air service development in N. Lancashire,* Maidenhead.
– (1970) *South Hampshire Airports Study,* for South Hampshire Plan Advisory Cttee.
– (1974) op. cit. Chap. 2.
White Papers and other government reports (1945) *British Air Services,* Cmd. **6712**.
– (1946) *London Airport. Report of the Layout Panel.*
– (1953) *London's Airports,* Cmd. **8902**.
– (1954) *Gatwick Airport.*
– (Reprint 1961), *Report of an Inquiry into the proposed development of Gatwick Airport,* Cmd. **9215**.
– (1961) *Civil aerodromes and air navigational services,* Cmd. **1457**.
– (1967) *The Third London Airport,* Cmd. **3259**.
– (1967) *Report of the Inquiry into local objections to the proposed development of land at Stansted as the Third Airport for London.*
– (1972) *Civil Aviation policy guidance,* Cmd. **4899**.
– (1957) *Report of the London Airport Development Committee* (Millbourn Cttee.)
– (1964) *Report of the Inter-departmental Cttee. on the Third London Airport,* CAP 1
– (1970) Commission on the Third London Airport op. cit. Chap. 2
– (1974) Department of Trade op. cit. Chap. 3.

5 Prospects for the future

The history of aviation in western countries since 1913 has been one of almost uninterrupted technical advance, spurred on by two major conflicts. The inter-war years were formative years for civil flying, a period when the market for air services lay with the businessman and the rich. Modern air transport came out of incubation after 1950, and since that time its markets have widened to take in, not only business interests, but tourists and family travel as well. The 'inclusive tour' explosion after 1963 has drawn in people of all ages with a wide range of incomes. The general trend has been upwards, averaging about 10–15 per cent a year for passenger traffic, and even the recession of 1958 and the years immediately following with the new jet airliners, produced only a hiccup in the curve. Indeed, for tour traffic and for air cargo, the rate of annual increase has topped 25 per cent on many routes. The atmosphere of continual growth bred a sense of optimism within the industry, both amongst airlines and airport authorities.

There were certainly contrary trends, but these have a much shorter history. Noise complaints around Heathrow showed their first real jump with the introduction of jets after 1959, and we have already seen what little account was officially taken of such matters in reports of that period (Inter-departmental Committee on the Third London Airport, CAP 199, 1964). I remember feeling inadequately informed when addressing audiences in Harlow and Bishop's Stortford on the environmental effects of airports in 1964, for little evidence was available for the U.K.; the major work at this time had been done by the Port of New York Authority (1960–61) in the U.S.A. As the feasibility of the supersonic airliner (S.S.T.) became clear, after early work in the 1950s (Morgan 1972) which led to the Concorde and the ill-fated U.S. designs of the Boeing company, anxiety became more widespread. There arose the possibility of pollution hazards from such aircraft flying at altitudes over 15 000 m. which offset the hopes of another quantum jump in Man's conquest of earth space. Traffic growth itself provided another source of worry as the queues of aircraft on the ground and in the air brought congestion to the major airports, particularly in the U.S.A. where the problem was first experienced. The current decade has brought the fuel crisis, and inflation. The price of jet fuel on the north Atlantic route has increased from 13·3 U.S. cents per gallon in April–June 1973, to 36·1 cents for the same period in 1974—an increase of.171 per cent. This has raised the critical issue of economy and efficiency in airline and airport operations. For air transport especially, congestion and high fuel prices are a crippling combination.

Society itself has changed since 1950, more particularly in Britain we have seen the apparently relentless march of urban society upon which aviation feeds. With it has come greater demands for intra, and inter-urban travel. Access to big airports, as we have seen, poses severe problems, and has encouraged the growth of 'commuter' airlines to link downtown strips with the ever-receding major airports; receding more in time than in actual distance. Such development makes new demands upon aircraft, and has forced attention less upon cruising efficiency, and more upon short-field performance, economy, and low noise levels. On the other hand, the rise of multi-national corporations with wide spatial contacts, has put a premiu on fast long and medium-haul services. Higher disposable incomes have favoured the rapid development of tourist travel, a market that has already penetrated the long-haul routes.

The future then will depend upon the emphasis placed upon each of these aspects of change which we must dwell upon in more detail. First, we begin with technology itself. Clarke (1973) has made the point that contemporary technology in the developed world is regarded as polluting. He then discusses several responses made to it, and these form an interesting background to our discussion. The responses are:

1. Price response. Pollution is the price we pay for advanced technology and it is well worth the price.

2. 'Fix-it' response. This school accepts the problem but sees no fundamental wrong in current technologies. They claim that serious action will restore the position. This means more technology not less, using sophisticat devices to monitor and control pollution.

3. 'Away-with-it' response. The price paid is too high.

4. Alternative response. Current technology is polluting, and cannot be changed, but not all technologies are like this. We need to develop new forr

5. Political response. Pollution results from the inventions of capitalist elites, and their exploitation of the people. Pollution is, then, a product, not a cause, and as such is not in itself important.

Clarke sees these responses as a matter of taste and philosophy, not subject to scientific analysis, and hence difficult to assess. Apart from this aspect, there are others. Thus present technology is capital-intensive and tends to be the prerogative of richer nations, or it uses scarce resources too rapidly— for example fossil fuels—or it is capable of misuse, i.e. the bomber may be substituted for the airliner in the case of aviation.

The future for airports is tied up with civil aviation's future, and here responses vary, though many seem to follow a 'fix-it' response in the indust itself. The quieter, widebody jets with their reduced noise 'footprints', and their better field performance using existing airports, are a first reaction to noise, as well as the need for economy. When it comes to the S.S.T., as epitomized by Concorde, responses tend to be more mixed. Airlines are cautious, wondering nervously about its operating costs when it once gets into operation. In 1974 British Airways reported that 'with the less buoyant world air transport market following the energy crisis, we shall be unable to absorb the adverse effect of Concorde from our subsonic operations' profits' (*Flight International*, 28 March 1974). Meanwhile, although the authorities are cautiously accepting Concorde, a public inquiry in New York currently discussing Concorde operations, looks like a victory for the anti-S.S.T. groups. Upper air research into the effects of S.S.T. jet efflux upon the ozone layer of the atmosphere has also produced varying results. Much seems to depend upon the number and the altitude at which the S.S.T.s will fly. An M.I.T. model (*Flight International*, 10 October 1974) showed that a fleet of 500 S.S.T.s flying at 18 200 m. could lead to a decrease in ozone of 16 per cent in the Northern Hemisphere, but other models ranged from 0·5 to 15·0 per cent. Operations at 16 700 m. could also reduce the figure by 3 to 4 per cent. The U.S. Department of Transportation, basing its remarks on a four-year study costing $40 million (climatic impact assessment program—C.I.A.P.) thought a small number of S.S.T.s, such as the sixteen proposed Concordes, together with fourteen Russian Tu 144 S.S.T.s, would not harm the Earth's environment (*Flight International*, 30 January 1975). Amongst other airline and airport authorities, views also differ. Mr. Lundberg, a former director of the Swedish Aeronautical Research Centre, considers that a safe, socially acceptable, and economic S.S.T. cannot be built (*Flight International* 4 April 1974), while Mr. Boyd-Carpenter, chairman of the C.A.A., has maintained that top people would require supersonic travel (*Financial Times* Conference 1974). Finally, a message sent to the Minister for Industry by the body representing aircraft industry technicians and shop-floor workers, said that to scrap Concorde now would be an act of gross betrayal by a Labour government pledged to protect the interests of the workers and the nation. Most of Clarke's responses are here, including perhaps a new one called 'political expediency'. More generally, Mr. Hammarskjold, director-general of the International Air Transport Association, thinks that the industry has not helped the present situation by rushing to take advantage of new technology for competitive rather than economic reasons. He considers that new technology would not, as in the past, solve the industry's problems.

With so much changing, he would be a brave man who thought he could confidently foresee the events of the next twenty-five years. However, some attempt must be made and for this purpose it is perhaps best to

consider the easier task of developments in the next few years, first,
before examining the longer term.

In the shorter term, we can expect the current fleets of the newer wide-
body jets to expand and take over the majority of services. The outlook
for traffic growth for them is less certain. Thus in 1974 traffic through
London's airports showed a decrease of 1·5 per cent over 1973 for passeng
traffic, and a 2·1 per cent drop in aircraft movements, and this is the first
decrease since 1945. Nor is this confined to London. The Paris airports
showed only a 1·0 per cent increase for the same period, compared with
previous levels of 12 per cent, while eleven West German airports only
managed a slightly better record with an average increase of 4·1 per cent
on traffic.

Under such economic conditions, no radical change in our airport syste
is likely in the short-term. At a conference on regional airports last year,
the director of Manchester airport told delegates that it might be too late
to formulate a total plan for regional airports, for not only must airport
expenditure compete with other sectors of industry, but rationalization of
these airports would meet opposition from large sections of the populatior
of those areas. However, there is room for improvement at regional levels.
The development of services from regional airports to our E.E.C. partners
is a recent trend that will surely grow in importance; indeed, British Airwa
have gone on record as saying that such services were a primary aim of
policy (*Flight International,* 16 Mary 1974). Within airport terminals, too,
recent surveys of passenger reaction showed dissatisfaction with baggage
handling—among other things—indicating room for improvement at no
great expense.

The Central England Study (p. 00) indicated the sort of rationalization
that might take place over a longer time span. Given a more more stable
economic situation, it is possible to give credence to attempts to construct
a series of solutions by model techniques, covering the whole country.
Such models might then be evaluated by cost-benefit studies and form the
basis for discussion with interested communities. Indeed, there is a case
for such studies to be undertaken now, even if their implementation is
progressive over time. Our relations within the E.E.C., and the degree of
rationalization of European airline networks, as well as airports, that migh
be warranted in the future, are all areas which should be covered by such
a study.

Moving on still further, we may speculate how far a need for economy
will alter technological response. In March 1975 the De Havilland aircraft
company of Canada (D.H.C.) first flew the 'Dash 7' feederliner. This 50-
seat, S.T.O.L. airliner, equipped with four turbo-propeller engines is aimed
at medium and high density commuter and regional carriers. It is a respons

to the need for a machine to operate from small (600 m.) airstrips near built-up areas at lower cost, and minimum nuisance. It is claimed that, over a 320 km stage, it will use 40 per cent less fuel per seat than a twin-engined jet, and that its noise level is 20 EPNdB below the United States noise regulations for new aircraft. This then appears to be a design based on economy rather than high cruising speed. Carried to its conclusion, such thinking will eventually reach true vertical take-off and landing (V.T.O. L.) aircraft. Because of the need for economy and minimum nuisance, such machines are not likely to be in service until the end of the century. For small countries like the U.K., it is debatable whether internal inter-city services should ever be handled by V.T.O.L. aircraft, or whether high speed surface transport is not more appropriate. However, for short-haul services between European cities, S.T.O.L. or V.T.O.L. aircraft make far more sense. High cruising speeds seem to be unnecessary, a level of 350–650 km per hour might be adequate. Nor will complicated terminals and ticket reservation systems be necessary, since such a system, to capture a mass inter-city market, must be simple for the customer to use. Boarding a 'Euroair' service in the future ought to be as easy as catching a train.

On long hauls, development will follow an evolutionary rather than a revolutionary path, according to Clay and Sigalla of the Boeing Aircraft Company (*Flight International,* 3 April 1975). They see the development of more efficient sub-sonic and S.S.T. airliners, with fuel consumptions reduced by 5–10 per cent over current models. If the N.A.S.A. 'quiet engine program' is any indication, they should be quieter too. Thus a current Douglas DC-8 generates 117 EPNdB at take-off and on the landing approach, compared with the Federal noise regulation (F.A.R. 36) limit of 106 EPNdB for new aircraft of equivalent size. A quiet engine fitted into an acoustically treated nacelle could reach 90 EPNdB on take-off, and 89 EPNdB on landing, according to this source. As far as fuel economy is concerned, studies for the use of liquid hydrogen, or ethanol (C_2H_2OH) which can be produced by solar energy from fermented cereal grain, have already begun. The eventual use of such benign fuels, which are pollution-free, depends upon the solution of many technical problems, not the least of which is the volume required to store the fuel on the aircraft. Their application in any case would be to aircraft similar to the Boeing 747. As yet there are no alternatives to the fixed wing aircraft that appear feasible, although the use of airships for cargo transport has been explored. Some schemes envisage these airships as remaining aloft for long periods, and perhaps loading from depots not dissimilar to present-day container terminals.

To bring these strands together in terms of an airport system is a fascinating speculation. Possibly we will see a limited number of major long-haul airports, each serving particular urban regions that may transcend national boundaries. These airports would be supported by a denser network of S.T.O.L. short-haul terminals connecting the component communities of our regions. Our future in any case is to sharpen our tools for the tasks imposed by the advent of such sophisticated systems. The Roskill Commission will probably be seen in the future as a prototype of many succeeding study groups concerned with air transport development. Perhap the philosopher A. N. Whitehead provides us with the most fitting conclusion, 'It is the business of the future to be dangerous; and it is among the merits of science that it equips the future for its duties. It must be admitte that there is a degree of instability which is inconsistent with civilization. But on the whole, the great ages have been unstable ages.'

Further reading

Allen, J. E. (1971) 'The future of aeronautics—dreams and realities', *Aeronaut. Jnl.*, 75, 587.

Cross, N. et al (1974) *Man-made futures*, London.

Marshall, E. E. (1971) 'STOL aircraft in future transport systems', *Aeronaut. Jnl.*, 75, 695.

Miller, R. H. (1971) 'Some air transportation concepts for the future', *Aeronaut. Jnl.* 75, 431.

Mowforth, E. (1971) 'A design study for a freight carrying airship', *Aeronaut. Jnl.*, 75, 166.

Royal Aeronatucial Society (1973) 'Symposium on heliports', *Aeronaut. Jnl.*, 77, 21

Steiner, J. E. (1970) 'Aircraft development and world aviation growth', *Aeronaut. Jnl.* 74, 433.

References

Clarke, R. (1973) 'The pressing need for alternative technology', *Impact of Science on Society*, 23.

Inter-Departmental Committee on the Third London Airport (1964) op. cit. Chap. 4 under White Paper and Reports.

Morgan, Sir Morien (1972) op. cit. Chap. 1.

Port of New York Authority (1960) *The economic relationship of air transport to the economy of the New Jersey—New York Metropolitan area*, C.E.I.R. Inc., New York.

– (1961) *Economic effects of a major airport, the New Jersey—New York Metropolitan area*, New York.